The Dam the Drought Built

A History of the South Saskatchewan River Project

The Dam the Drought Built

A History of the South Saskatchewan River Project

by Max Macdonald

CANADIAN PLAINS RESEARCH CENTER

1999

Canadian Plains Research Center
University of Regina
Regina, Saskatchewan S4S 0A2
Canada

email: canadian.plains@uregina.ca
http://www.cprc.uregina.ca

Canadian Cataloguing in Publication Data

Macdonald, Max, 1920-

      The dam the drought built

      ISBN 0-88977-136-7

1. South Saskatchewan River Project–History. 2. Water
resources development–Saskatchewan–History.
3. Saskatchewan–History–1945- I. University
of Regina. Canadian Plains Research Center. II. Title.

TD227.S37M33 1999   333.91'3'0971242   C99-920226-X

Cover Design: Donna Achtzehner, Canadian Plains Research Center

Printed and bound in Canada by
Houghton Boston, Saskatoon, Saskatchewan

Printed on acid-free paper.

— Dedication —

Mother and Bannie
and
Kathleen, Heather, Ellen and Douglas

Table of Contents

Acknowledgements...viii

Introduction...1

Chapter 1: Wasteland or Treasure Trove?..3

Chapter 2: A Cry for Help: From Crisis to Action......................................15

Chapter 3: The Political Struggle Begins...27

Chapter 4: "A Dam Site Surer and a Dam Site Sooner".........................39

Chapter 5: "Irrigate or Migrate"..45

Chapter 6: A New Face for a Storied Stream 61

Chapter 7: Bringing in the Sheaves 85

Epilogue 97

Notes...100

Acknowledgements

The author is indebted to so many who gave so freely of their time and support. In particular there is the staff of the Canadian Plains Research Center who provided both advice and funding for this project, including Dr. James McCrorie, Dr. David Gauthier, Brian Mlazgar, Donna Achtzehner and Lorraine Nelson. Also providing financial support was the Saskatchewan Heritage Foundation for which I am most grateful. There were the staff members of SaskWater, who added invaluable background information, especially Harvey Fjeld, Alex Banga, Bryan Ireland, Al Veroba and the staff at the Outlook office, along with the past and present cast of the Prairie Farm Rehabilitation Administration including Dr. Harry Hill, J. Gordon Watson, William Berry, Bert Lukey, Dawson Young, and Brad Fairley, and the library staff who were extremely helpful in finding obscure documents.

Staff members of the Saskatchewan Archives were most helpful and those at the University of Regina library were also of assistance. The extraordinary efforts of the staff of the Diefenbaker Centre were also much appreciated, particularly the efforts of Dr. Bruce Shepard and Naoise Johnson. The libraries of the two largest Saskatchewan daily newspapers, the *Star-Phoenix*, and the *Leader-Post* also were helpful. A special thanks to Con Rumold and to Frank Roy.

Those directly involved in some of the spin-offs from the project must be thanked for their forthright observations, including the Larson brothers, Arnold and Edgar, and the other set of brothers — Robert and Merle — bearing the same surname. There was also another Larson named Arlo who lent minutes and other papers of the activities of the Irrigation Investigation Group which aided in the understanding of that particular body. Doug Barker and Bob Tullis of Lucky Lake helped untangle the intricacies of the potato industry in that village.

The views of Tommy Hamilton must be acknowledged posthumously; his philosophy of farming was extremely useful in putting many of the other factors into context. There, too, were the residents of Dunblane, Harold and Pat Stavenjord and former mayor, Len Bartzen, who shed light on life in the village. Among the entrepreneurs who provided help were Bill Childerhose and Harry Meyers of Barrich farms, Greg Sommerfeld and Glen Gordon. Wayne Vermette was a great contributor, supplying copies of reports and studies, along with his own observations

Introduction

The story of the South Saskatchewan River Project, with the subsequent construction of the Gardiner Dam and Lake Diefenbaker, is as deeply etched into the Saskatchewan psyche as it is into the Saskatchewan landscape. Its genesis antedates the birth of the province, and its legacy continues to be felt by a majority of Saskatchewan's citizens to this day.

Born out of the despair generated by the disastrous drought of the 1930s, the dam project was controversial from the very beginning. The studies and discussions which preceded its eventual construction were accompanied by a level of infighting which surprised even those who were accustomed to this province's raucous political climate. There were those who opposed the dam as unrealistic, uneconomical, a pipe dream. Others supported the project, but wished to reap the benefits at the polls, and were unwilling to share the limelight with their political opponents. Liberals, Conservatives, and CCF/NDP — party loyalties were divided by the project. And finally, when the dam was constructed, there was an effort at reconciliation, as the contributions of men of all political persuasions were recognized: Gardiner Dam, named for James G. (Jimmy) Gardiner, the Liberal premier who fought long and hard for the project, and who died before its completion; Lake Diefenbaker, for John G. Diefenbaker, the Conservative prime minister who made the construction of the dam one of his electoral platforms, and Douglas Park, for T.C. Douglas, the CCF premier who was also a long-time supporter of the dam.

The principal players are all gone now, and history will be the ultimate judge of their political sparring. Only the dam itself remains. The dam, and the controversy surrounding its construction.

Ultimately, should it have been built? Perhaps, and then again, perhaps not. Again, history must be the judge. We are still too close in time to the dam's completion to be able to fairly assess all of its impacts on Saskatchewan: economic, social, and environmental.

Could it be built today? Probably not. In an age of environmental lobby groups, budgetary restraint, the retreat of "big government," and rampant "individualism," it would be difficult, if not impossible, to undertake a project of this magnitude. And yet, it was done. Saskatchewan, traditionally a "have-not" province, was able to marshall the political will and the financial resources to build the dam — the second-largest construction project in Canadian history.

Mistakes were undoubtedly made. But we must be careful not to judge too harshly the proponents of the dam with the wisdom of hindsight. Construction of the project began some forty years ago. In the intervening decades, we have learned much about science, the economy, and the environment. Should things have been done differently? Assuredly. However, what cannot be doubted is the sincerity of those who supported the dam, and fought for its construction — their heartfelt desire to improve the lives of the citizens of this province.

This, then, is the story of "The Dam the Drought Built."

— ONE —

Wasteland or Treasure Trove?

The South Saskatchewan River begins with a few crystalline droplets high in the Rocky Mountains and ends in the chill briny waters of Hudson Bay. Midway between these damp extremes, having been brought to maturity by the flows of the Oldman, Bow and Red Deer rivers, its turbulent rush has been halted by a massive barrier of millions of tons of earth and concrete designed to turn it into a source of survival for the inhabitants of one of Canada's most arid settled regions. The decision by Prime Minister John G. Diefenbaker's Conservative government in 1958 to tap the life-giving waters of the river by means of a dam came only after a chain of events reaching back a century. Drought and hail, rust and frost, grasshoppers and Russian thistle, hard-working but unskilled farmers, settlement patterns, railway construction, international commodity prices, industrial development and political manoeuverings — all played roles in aiding or hampering attempts to use these waters to enrich life in a region which had been alternately viewed as the breadbasket of the world or the dustbowl of despair.

The Gardiner Dam, completed in 1967, sits near the upper fringes of a portion of the Prairies known as the Palliser Triangle. Captain John Palliser, who explored the area in 1857, saw it as part of the great American desert protruding into Canada, the boundaries of which he set as "its base the 49th parallel from longitude 100 degrees to 114 degrees west, with its apex reaching to the 52nd parallel of latitude."[1] He declared the region to be "desert or semi-desert in character, which can never be expected to become occupied by settlers."[2] John Macoun, who traversed the country a decade later, held that:

> We have then, a dry, clear, cold winter, a dry spring with bright sunshine; a warm summer with an abundance of rain… . An atmosphere like this… causes me to feel…that our great North-West is truly a land of "illimitable possibilities."[3]

The roots of these conflicting views, which were to bedevil several generations of residents to follow, lay in the capricious nature of the land. This was illustrated more than three quarters of a century later by the man whose name the dam now bears. James G. (Jimmy) Gardiner, a Saskatchewan farmer and then premier of the province, speaking before the Empire Club of Toronto on March 8, 1935 said:

> We are continually working between two difficult possibilities, Drought and Rust or Frost… we get the necessary amount of moisture more often than we are compelled to do without.

> What has prairie experience shown? 1. In those sections of the country settled before 1890 there was drought from 1890 to 1895. 2. In 1907 the crop was frozen. 3. 1914 was the driest year we ever had. 4. 1917 to 1921

Facing page: the Palliser Triangle area of Saskatchewan. (map produced by Information Systems Division, Canadian Plains Research Center)

Below: Captain John Palliser (1818-1887). Photo courtesy Saskatchewan Archives Board (SAB) — R-A4962(1).

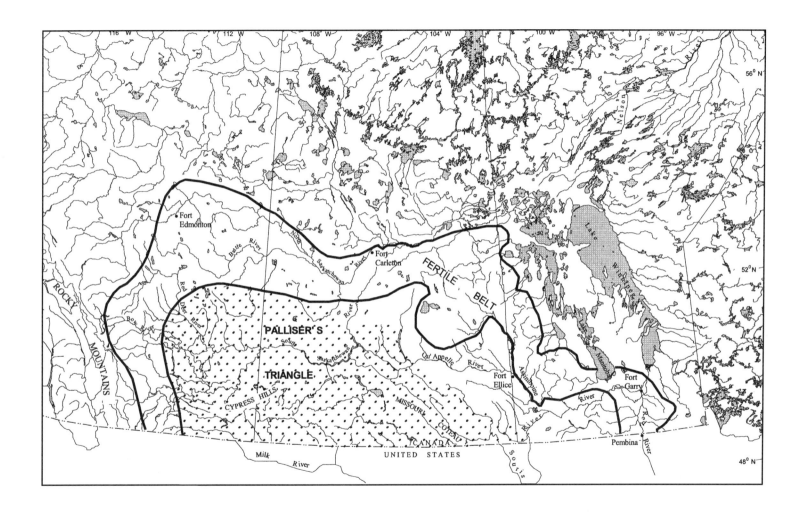

was as dry in certain areas as the present period.

To recall the drought of the 90s is to recall the good crop years between 1900 and 1914. To recall 1914, the worst year in our history, is to recall 1915 and 1916, the best years in the history of the southwest. To recall the years from 1917 to 1921 is to recall the years from 1922 to 1928, the years of bumper crops and good prices. That is why we are "next-year" country.[4]

Elaborating on this theme, the premier noted that in the years 1926-28 the value of farm products was $1.18 billion, but in the years 1931-33 the value was $354 million. The three best years produced more than three times the value of the three worst. The poor crops, of course, stemmed from low moisture and resultant blowing dust. He went on to declare: "All that is required to stop dust blowing and produce wheat again is rain."[5]

Gardiner pointed out that long-term averages were able to sustain good crop production. But Edgar Carlson, an Outlook farmer who grew up in the area during the 1930s and was among the first to embrace irrigation when it became available, said in a 1995 interview: "If you get a long-term average of about 14 inches but get half of that for five years running the average isn't worth a damn," adding with a wry smile, "but maybe worth a dam."[6]

Gardiner, by tracing the vagaries of the area, did much to explain the apparently contradictory views of Palliser and Macoun: quite simply, they visited the area at different times. Recent studies carried out by Roslyn A. Case and Glen M. MacDonald illustrate

John Macoun (1831-1920).
Photo courtesy SAB — R-A4897.

that these cycles have been present in the region for more than four centuries.[7]

Pushing West

Despite Palliser's negative report, a federal government initiative in 1872 was to provide the impetus for widespread settlement. In that year,

two pieces of legislation were passed by Parliament to facilitate and expedite the settlement of the newly acquired Northwest. The Dominion Lands Act, which went through a number of alterations and amendments later, established three basic provisions. A settler might take up a quarter-section of unoccupied Dominion land upon the payment of a $10 registration fee to prove up on it as a free homestead. After three years, he might file a claim of ownership if he could show proof that he had carried out his residential duties and had broken a specified number of acres. A companion statute, the Immigration and Colonization Act, set up various ways of attracting settlers. It provided for recruiting agents to be sent abroad and for publicity campaigns to be launched. After the passage of these two measures, the Canadian government waited optimistically for an inrush of settlers.[8]

A generation later, these measures were to bear fruit:

Within a single decade of the Saskatchewan Act of 1905 the area patented for homesteads in that province had risen from 2,780,000 acres to 21,500,000 acres…. It was recognized on all sides that the free-homestead system was serving a far-reaching purpose in the settlement of Western Canada.[9]

Most likely oblivious to the views of both Palliser and Macoun, and to the unpredictability of the climate, settlers arrived in record numbers. Between 1901 and 1906, the population in seven census divisions in the southwest portion of the province swelled from 8,253 to 52,505, ultimately peaking at 313,673 in 1931.[10] The increase in population brought rapid increases in grain production. Acreages seeded to wheat in this area tripled in the same five years, while production increased more than seven times. By 1928, the province's farmers had sown near 14,000,000 acres to wheat and produced 321,215,000 bushels — more than ninety times the output in 1900.[11]

A "Sad Shock" for Many

There were several reasons why so many came and why the government was eager to populate the west. First, settlement was necessary to protect the land from seizure by the Americans; equally important, the western hinterland was to provide raw materials to, and serve as a market for, Britain and eastern Canada. In 1908 Clifford Sifton, the Minister of the Interior, said:

> the interest of the Dominion in the lands is in the revenue which it can derive from the settler who makes that land productive… . it has made millions out of these lands without selling an acre… The increase in our customs returns, the increase in our trade and commerce, the increase in our manufactures, is to a very large extent due to the increase in settlement on the free lands of the Northwest Territories. … It is worth the while of the Dominion to spend hundreds of thousands of dollars in promoting immigration… .[12]

According to A.S. Morton, the "most potent influences" driving the swift westward push of the rail lines were

> the desire of the Dominion Government to realize on its lands, the pressure of the land agents for the development of their districts, and the desire of the Canadian Pacific Railway to sell its lands. The settlers were the pawns in the game.[13]

Many years later, Jimmy Gardiner would argue that as repayment for benefits it had derived from these policies at the expense of those who lived in the region, the Dominion government should contribute liberally to the South Saskatchewan River Project.

The settlers who arrived in great numbers often found that the land was not at all what they had expected, or what they had been led to expect. Nancy Powell of Southey, interviewed on the occasion of her 102nd birthday, recalled that settlement promoters had shown her parents photographs of the lush, well-treed lands of the Ontario countryside, passing them off as from Saskatchewan. Her parents were aghast when they arrived on the nearly treeless plains north of Regina.[14]

Others were misled by their own families. Howard Dean, whose family ties are rooted in the pioneer days of rural southwestern Saskatchewan, said that one of his forebears came west from Ontario and erected a sod shack on his quarter section homestead, then sent back east for his bride. She apparently had misinterpreted just what a sod shack looked like. It appears she had envisioned some romantic little dwelling, but upon encountering the primitive nature of her future home declared, "This sod shack is a sad shock," picked up her belongings and headed back to Ontario, never to return.

Such conditions were overlooked by others who valued land ownership above all hardships — such a prize was beyond their dreams in their homelands. Others approached the open plains from a more practical level. Kenneth McDonald, with a brood of seven children on a small Ontario farm, came west to explore larger fields in 1909. According to his son, Hugh, he checked out northern Saskatchewan and parts of Alberta before landing in Glenside, Saskatchewan, where he bought a section of land because it was all but devoid of trees. Unlike many settlers, he saw this lack of trees as a virtue which allowed him to get into production without the bother of clearing land. The farm still remains in the family in the hands of the widow of his grandson and her two children.

The South Saskatchewan River: An Answer to the Problem

But wherever they came from, and whatever their initial reactions to the land, all settlers would eventually be confronted with the periodic droughts to which Gardiner had referred in his Toronto speech. During each of these dry periods there was a new spate of discussions on how to deal with the problem.

The first known proponent of turning the waters of the South Saskatchewan to more useful ends had been Henry Youle Hind, who explored the region in 1858, a year after Palliser. Hind was searching for a transportation route to the west. He envisaged a steamboat route from Fort Garry to the Rockies, made possible by diverting the South Saskatchewan by means of a dam near its elbow. This, he said, would move the water down the Qu'Appelle into the Assiniboine and thence into the Red. Hind calculated the details of the dam with some precision: "a dam 58 feet high, and 600 to 800 yards long … across a deep, narrow valley in which the south branch flows below where the Qu'Appelle valley joins it."[15]

Though the transportation proposal was rejected in favour of a rail line, Hind's expanded views of the potential of this river were prophetic when he suggested:

> The time may yet arrive when the future population of Rupert's Land and the Dakotah territory will find it advantageous to construct … [dams or spillways linking the South Saskatchewan with the Qu'Appelle] or similar works, even if they should be for the purposes of irrigation or inland navigation.[16]

Thus was planted, long before newcomer settlement, the seed for any number of future schemes to tap into the waters of the South Saskatchewan near the headwaters of the Qu'Appelle.

George Spence — variously a Saskatchewan farmer, member of the Legislative Assembly, member of Parliament, director of the Prairie Farm Rehabilitation Administration, and member of the

Henry Youle Hind (1823-1908). Copy of a picture in the London Illustrated News, *October 2, 1858. Photo courtesy SAB — R-A4896.*

International Joint Commission (on water) — was closely associated with Saskatchewan's water problems, and discussed several attempts to deal with the problem in his book, *Survival of a Vision*. He noted that although there were several approaches to solving the problem, most envisaged the South Saskatchewan as essential to any solution. Spence focussed on what was to become a recurring theme in all attempts to solve the water problem:

> the Dominion government … never relaxed in its efforts to find some feasible means of diverting water from the only known source of unlimited supply — the South Saskatchewan River.
>
> For such information as was available, at the time, on the proposal to divert water from the South Saskatchewan, credit rightly goes to a few senior officials of the Irrigation Branch, Department of the Interior, who were the first to conduct surveys and investigations in the area.[17]

In particular, Spence acknowledged the work of J.S. Dennis and William Pearce, both Dominion Land Surveyors, who, in the two decades before the turn of the century, urged a common goal of "artificial application of water for crop production in the low rainfall area of the Territories."[18]

Dennis also made important contributions to the drafting of the *North-West Irrigation Act* (1894), which was intended to "provide for careful supervision by the Government of the first distribution and the subsequent use of available water supply in the arid region."[19] He proposed a canal, some 55 miles upstream from Aitkow Creek, which would feed some of the South Saskatchewan waters into the Qu'Appelle by force of gravity. The plan was found to be unworkable because the decline was not steep enough to move the water freely. The impracticability of this approach shifted attention to a number of alternate schemes involving the employment of pump lifts, cuts, tunnels, canals, pipelines and dams designed to get the South Saskatchewan waters to some point where they could be fed into the parched lands to the south.

Other studies into the water problem were also underway. In 1907, Regina launched an examination of its water problems. The city had grown swiftly during the first decade of the century — from 2,300 in 1901 to 30,000 by 1911. The study concluded that local supply sources would not meet future needs and suggested a possible feed from the South Saskatchewan. In 1911, Moose Jaw hired an engineer from Montreal to explore a source to meet its needs. He, too, pinpointed the South Saskatchewan as the only viable water source. Later, a consultant to the federal public health department concluded that "the whole of the district … must remain limited in growth unless a visible water supply can be obtained" and that "the only apparent available and practically unlimited supply was from the South Saskatchewan River."[20] He added that possible schemes to make this water available would be best handled by a commission, coordinated by the provincial government, representing all municipalities within the region. In time, this suggestion in somewhat revised form led to a broad-based attempt to solve the problem.

First Attempts at a Solution

In 1911, federal authorities presented two approaches to provide water for the cities of Regina and Moose Jaw, and some nearby communities: a link from the South Saskatchewan and Aitkow creek into the Qu'Appelle; and a route about thirty miles upstream at Shellstone Creek into Thunder Creek. Though this latter plan was discarded at the time, a modified version played a minor but important role in the creation of a wetland bird refuge after the South Saskatchewan River Project was completed. The first plan included a dam across the river with a hydroelectric plant capable of providing enough power to pump water from the river to a sufficient height to clear the summit into the Qu'Appelle valley and create a gravity feed into Buffalo Pound Lake as a holding reservoir. Interestingly, the question of the environmental impact of this scheme was raised by F.H. Peters, commissioner of irrigation. He noted that "water diverted from the river [by a natural water course] must necessarily be liable to more or less serious contamination,"[21] and proposed a filter bed to purify the water. With the declaration of war in August 1914 this project was shelved.

In 1919 (in the midst of the 1917-21 drought), the provincial government convened a conference to explore the water matter again. It was attended by Premier William M. Martin and other government officials and representatives of Regina, Moose Jaw, and a number of surrounding communities. Speaking on behalf of the districts, G.D. Mackie, Moose Jaw city commissioner, urged the provincial government to help both in organizing and financing a scheme to secure water for "domestic, industrial, manufacturing, railway and farming purposes."[22]

The premier balked at the notion of the province bankrolling the scheme, noting that it would be unfair for the province to pay for a huge project which would, in effect, benefit only one region at the expense of others. Thus it was agreed that the undertaking should be self-supporting, with each district being expected to pay for what it received. This decision formed the basis for a water tax which caused some political turbulence when irrigation was introduced on a large scale many years later. The premier did agree, later that year, to set up a commission to establish pipeline routes and water district structures, through *An Act Respecting the Supply of Water from the South Saskatchewan River* (1919-20).

The commission's report set forth details of the working of a plan that involved a pipeline directly from the South Saskatchewan River to Regina, with spurs to serve surrounding areas. In accordance with clause 5 of the *Act*, a vote by all municipal electors in the region was conducted in 1921. The cities voted in favour, but the smaller communities were opposed and the scheme was dropped. However, another search was launched by Regina in 1928 and a report was tabled in city council in 1930. This study examined the possibility of using Long Lake, the Qu'Appelle lakes and Moose Mountain Lake as sources; it was concluded that all were impractical, and that the South Saskatchewan was the only viable source. Although it was acknowledged that a solution to the problem would reap rich rewards, the project was shelved because of the cost.

During his speech in Toronto, Gardiner had remarked that if a worthwhile solution to a major problem were found, the money would also be found. Obviously the water problem was not yet urgent enough. However, circumstances would soon elevate the situation from the category of a mere worry to a full-scale panic.

— TWO —

A Cry for Help: From Crisis to Action

In 1933, Conservative Prime Minister R.B. Bennett received this letter from a farm woman living west of Saskatoon:

> It is with a very humble heart I take the opportunity of writing this letter to … ask you if you will please send for the underware in the Eaton order (made out and enclosed in this letter). My husband will be 64 in Dec. and has nuritis very bad at times in his arms and shoulders. We have had very little crop for the last three years, not enough at all to pay taxes and live and this year crops around here … are a complete failure. My husband is drawing wood on the waggon for 34 miles and had to draw hay too, for feed for horses, this winter. He has to take two days for a trip and sleep under the waggon sometimes. He is away for wood today and it is cold and windy… . I have patched and darned his old underware for the last two years; but they are completely done now, if you cant do this I really dont know what to do. We have never asked for anything of anybody before, we seem to be shut out from the world altogether — we have

no telephone Radio or newspaper. For the last couple of years we … could not afford to have them. We used to enjoy your speeches on the Radio also the Sunday church services, as we cant get out very much in winter. If I can only get this underware for my husband I can manage for myself in some way. He has to be out in the cold, where I can stay in the house… .[1]

Bennett's secretary replied:

> … While you can realize Mr. Bennett has been inundated with similar requests, nevertheless in view of the health of your husband I have forwarded to the T. Eaton Co. Limited, order for high grade, heavyweight Wolsey underwear… . I trust you will treat this matter as strictly confidential… .[2]

This plea for the purchase of an item listed at $5.95 in the *Eaton's Catalogue* reflects the plight of thousands of families struggling to survive in a land which they had entered with such high hopes. That this woman was not alone is illustrated by statistics gathered by eighteen rural municipalities in the area. The statistics show that the "dried out bonus" (under the *Prairie Farm Assistance Act*) was paid in eight of ten years in the Rosedale Municipality and that "during the worst drought period of the 1930's approximately 99% of the Rosedale population was on relief."[3] As historian A.S. Morton noted:

> The story of the settlement of the Northwest begins with an ignorant optimism, passes on to disillusionment and even to despair… . Looked at in one light, the history of the settlement of the West is a phase of the long struggle of man to conquer nature.[4]

The Dirty Thirties: When "Next Year" Never Came

In his speech to the Toronto Empire Club in 1935 (see Chapter 1) Jimmy Gardiner explained the history of fluctuation between good times and bad in

R.B. Bennett (1870-1947) was Canada's eleventh prime minister from 1930-35. Photo courtesy SAB — S-B5093.

The Saskatchewan Relief Commission responded to the drought of the 1930s by issuing emergency relief orders for basic goods. Photo courtesy SAB — R-B2465(1).

prairie agriculture. The droughts were of relatively short duration and were preceded and followed by years of good to bumper crops; at one point he suggested that if farmers anticipated having one good crop in three, they could survive in comfort. As that infamous decade unfolded, however, the climate failed to fluctuate and instead proceeded into a downward spiral. The devastating impact of this lengthy drought was further aggravated by unsophisticated tillage methods, high winds, low wheat prices, crop diseases and grasshopper infestations. Had Prime Minister Bennett's secretary not responded to the farm woman's request for underwear, her husband might well have been waiting for it for many more years.

The drought of the 1930s was unprecedentedly long, and annual precipitation fell to record low levels. For example, according to Environment Canada records, the town of Outlook, which had normal rainfall of 315 mm, recorded a mere 108.6 mm in 1936 — the lowest on record.

In a paper presented at a prairie drought workshop in 1988, R.B. Godwin summarized the drought's catastrophic effects:

The drought of the 1930s is still regarded as the definitive drought in terms of designing structural solutions. In combination with a major economic depression, it intensified the poverty and hardships of prairie residents and forced a quarter of a million people to leave the prairies. It was a major drought by any definition; a meteorological drought because massive precipitation deficits were observed throughout the

R.M. ....225......

Saskatchewan Relief Commission
EMERGENCY RELIEF ORDER
1932-33

Nº 19401 MA

REGINA .....April 15-1933.....

Authority is hereby given to .......W.B. Law....... of .....Prairie River, Sask..... to deliver Food, Staple Groceries, Fuel, as set out on the reverse side

to the value of ....- - - - - -Ten - - - - - -....... Dollars, $10.00.......

To ......Walter Brooke Wright,..........   SASKATCHEWAN RELIEF COMMISSION

P.O. .....Prairie River, Sask.....

Sec.   Tp.   Rge.   W.   Mer.   Relief Officer

Not good after 30 days from date of issue
Merchants will send these orders to the Saskatchewan Relief Commission, Regina, for payment.

THIS ORDER MUST NOT BE PRESENTED THROUGH A BANK.

I hereby acknowledge receipt of the merchandise set out on the reverse side, in the quantities, qualities, and at the prices stated. All of which is satisfactory.   Date.........................

                                        I hereby certify that the merchandise specified on the reverse side hereof was this day delivered to the person to whom this order was issued in the quantities, and at the prices specified.

Walter Brooke Wright
            Applicant   Merchant

            Pay the amount of this order to

_____

_____

                                        Merchant

17

This Must Not Happen Again

These drawing by Harry Gutkin are a grim reminder of Saskatchewan agriculture during the "Hungry 30s" when the devastation of soil erosion was added to the burdens of the Depression. Photo courtesy SAB — R-B10963.

Right: A familiar sight in the 1930s: horses pulling a "Bennett Buggy" along a drifted-in road. Photo courtesy SAB — R-A4823.

18

entire prairie area, a hydrological drought because surface water and ground water resources showed major deficiencies and an agricultural drought because for a period in the 1930s virtually nothing grew. Lastly, it was a socio-economic drought, one that devastated both life-styles and financial capabilities of the prairie region of Canada.[5]

Overwhelmed as the prairie region was by this unprecedented catastrophe, the first steps toward a solution for coping with the unpredictability of the prairie climate were already being taken. Even as Jimmy Gardiner explained the dilemma of prairie farmers to the Empire Club in 1935, the Conservative government of R.B. Bennett was putting the final touches to the *Prairie Farm Rehabilitation Act* (PFRA), which would, in time, return much of the prairie wasteland to useful production. Ultimately, the agency created by this act became the pivotal force in bringing the South Saskatchewan River Project (SSRP) to life.

The First Step Taken: The *Prairie Farm Rehabilitation Act*

The *Prairie Farm Rehabilitation Act* was viewed by James Gray as "one of the most constructive pieces of legislation [the Bennett Government] ever passed."[6] A crucial function of the *Act* was to provide for the rehabilitation of drought and soil drifting areas in the provinces of Manitoba, Saskatchewan and Alberta. Under the minister of Agriculture an advisory committee was established, consisting of one representative of grain-growing farmers from the soil-drifting and drought regions of each of the three provinces, one representative of livestock farmers from the drought areas of Alberta and Saskatchewan, a member from each of the Mortgage Companies of Canada and the Canadian Bankers Association, one from each of the two major railways, two representatives from the Dominion Department of Agriculture, and one representative from each of the provincial governments. The duties of this committee were:

> to advise the minister as to the best methods to be adopted to secure the rehabilitation of the drought and soil drifting areas ... and to develop and promote within those areas systems of farm practice, tree culture and water supply that will afford greater economic security... .[7]

The act was originally intended to last for five years, but before that time had elapsed the Bennett government had been replaced by the Liberals under W.L. Mackenzie King. Jimmy Gardiner, who had moved from provincial to federal politics, was appointed minister of Agriculture responsible for the PFRA. In a report some years later to the Privy Council, Gardiner stated that the Liberals had felt from the beginning that the original *Act* was not going far enough and consequently it was broadened by amendments in 1937:

James Gardiner (1883-1962), premier of Saskatchewan from 1926-29 and 1934-35 and federal minister of Agriculture (1935-1957) under W.L. Mackenzie King. Photo courtesy SAB — R-A6030.

> We dropped the idea that this was to be only an effort to teach provincial and municipal authorities ... how to rehabilitate themselves and accepted the claim that the Federal treasury should help bear the cost ... over a period of years sufficiently long to accomplish the task in such a manner and to such an extent as would be reasonable.... [the amended] act provided for resettlement and the setting up of staffs of engineers and farm specialists who could plan rehabilitation.[8]

This core of engineers would later play a major role in setting the stage for the creation of the SSRP.

Under Gardiner's guidance and aided by the research in hand and the conscription of many staff members of the previously established experimental farms, the infant agency focussed on halting soil erosion and conserving what little moisture was available. Huge tracts of wind-swept land were seeded to crested wheat grass, previously nurtured by scientists at the University of Saskatchewan and the experimental farms from a small package of seed which had come originally from Russia.

George Spence, first director of the Prairie Farm Rehabilitation Administration from 1938-1947. This photo was taken in February 1964 at the closure of the South Saskatchewan River dam. Photo courtesy SAB — R-A16435 (2).

The agency urged the planting of shelter belts and encouraged radical changes in tillage methods in an attempt to combat the prevailing westerly winds.

This new agency was headed by George Spence, a dryland farmer and a member of the Saskatchewan Legislative Assembly. As the first director of the PFRA in 1938 his appointment was important in two respects. First, the creation of the position of director served to elevate the PFRA from a junior role in the Department of Agriculture into a full-fledged agency. Second, Spence himself was seen as the ideal candidate for the position. An Orkney Islander, with some 30 years experience as a dryland farmer, Spence had served both as a member of Parliament and a member of the Saskatchewan Legislative Assembly, and was noted for his tenacity. He once described the state of his farm when he first settled on it in 1912 as "cowless, henless, and treeless." To rectify one of these shortcomings he walked some 80 miles to the nearest railway siding, picked up about 1,600 seedlings and marched back to the farm to plant them. It was this type of energy which was to characterize his tenure as director of the PFRA.

Spence pushed for the creation of major irrigation projects, of which the South Saskatchewan River Project (SSRP) was to be the greatest. According to historian James Gray:

[I]t was no easy task for a non-engineer like Spence to recruit the staff of graduate engineers the organization needed, to say nothing of the lawyers and architects and accountants that were required…. Yet recruit [them he] did, and in the process he infected it with his own vision of the PFRA as a miracle-working organization that would transform the whole of the Palliser triangle from a disaster-prone distressed area into a Garden of Eden. It was Spence who converted the South Saskatchewan project from an engineering feasibility study into a social crusade.[9]

William Lyon Mackenzie King (1874-1950), prime minister for almost 22 years between 1921 and 1948. Photo courtesy SAB — R-B8254.

Spence took some encouragement for this "social crusade" from an experience he had had prior to his appointment to the PFRA, when he was part of a Saskatchewan delegation which met with Prime Minister King in 1937. Spence considered the following conversation "proof that the federal government was hospitable to large scale irrigation projects":

> "I wonder how long this terrible situation will continue?" the Prime Minister said, more as a thought ... than a question.... "[I]s there anything practical that can be done, in a large way, that would prevent ... the distress and hardship which these occasional severe droughts bring about over such a large area of the prairie provinces? I understand ... that there are possibilities of storing immense quantities of water by means of large dams in the rivers, and that this stored water could be used for the production of grain and other crops, thus offsetting the worst effects of these droughts. Are such projects feasible?" he asked anxiously. "Yes," I replied, "there are such possibilities but the projects would indeed be very large. The construction of them would take time and the costs would be high, very high." ... "Undoubtedly," he replied. "But the costs of relief are also high, and offer no permanent solution whatever of the problem."[10]

Spence was convinced that this conversation with King was a crucial step toward a more vigorous examination of water management beyond the dugouts, small dams and improved tillage practices which had already been initiated. It was, however, a step which had little immediate impact on the Saskatchewan scene as the PFRA itself was struggling toward maturity and attempting to maintain the momentum for small projects and some major works in Alberta.

The Search for a Site

While one might be tempted to focus on individuals, small groups or a few significant events which made the South Saskatchewan River Project feasible, it is essential to realize that the project emerged from the aspirations of scores of persons and events which eventually were to give it a life of its own. There were certainly the observations of Palliser, Hind and Macoun. There was the frustration of hundreds of farmers and politicians in their attempts to deal with the fluctuating water supplies during the first decades of settlement capped by the devastation of the 1930s. As a result of these events, many came to realize that such "next year country" swings would continue. Subsequently, some of those people placed themselves in positions to act as conduits to political figures who, in turn, could "make things happen." In particular, George Spence and his staff at the PFRA provided Jimmy Gardiner with the information he required to get sufficient funds for preliminary surveys in 1943, to search for a site for the dam and to assess the suitability of nearby lands for irrigation.

This search was aided by the fact that considerable work concerning funding responsibilities had already been done and information about the area was already available. As well, Spence consulted C.A. Magrath, a former Lethbridge area member of Parliament and former chairman of the International Joint Commission; Magrath had been actively involved in irrigation projects in the Lethbridge area and was recognized for his broad knowledge of the subject of large-scale uses for abundant water supplies. He believed that the federal government should construct large water storage projects and bear the entire cost, since the water would come from rivers which moved across provincial boundaries and therefore could not be considered within the jurisdiction of any single province. The St. Mary and Milk Rivers Development in Alberta (initiated in the early 1940s) was important in that the committee's set of recommendations to the federal government included some basic principles on division of costs and responsibilities which would later guide similar projects, including the SSRP.[11]

The William Pearce Stockwatering Project, proposed at nearly the same time, called for

> the diversion of the waters from the North Saskatchewan River, near Rocky Mountain House, into the Clearwater River, and from the Clearwater into the Red Deer River. From the Red Deer River the waters would be again diverted at a prescribed elevation, and thence conveyed by canals and natural water channels through a dry portion of east-central Alberta into west-central Saskatchewan as far east as the City of Saskatoon, thus serving something in the order of 1,400,000 acres for such purposes as stockwatering, irrigation and domestic supply.[12]

It was concluded that, at a cost of $74.84 per acre, the Pearce Project was prohibitively expensive and it was shelved. However, it did contain much information that would be useful to Spence and others when they were preparing plans for the SSRP.

A Site is Found

In the spring of 1943, PFRA engineers explored the region of Antelope Creek as a possible construction site. Spence had his staff prepare the data, which included preliminary investigations and geological information from Dr. J.A. Allan, a recognized authority on the geology of the region, who had explored the river by boat in 1917, in order to determine the feasibility of constructing a dam on the South Saskatchewan River for the purposes of irrigation. Spence personally took the request to Ottawa to plead for the funds to go ahead; funding was approved by Order in Council on January 21, 1944. Over the next six months, stability tests were conducted at six different sites within a thirteen-mile stretch bracketing Antelope Creek near Cabri. The results were conclusive:

> The material obtained as a result of a rather thorough reconnaissance of the area indicates quite definitely that the area is not suitable for any large-scale irrigation development as proposed in connection with this project.[13]

While the tests were disappointing, Spence noted that "there was no thought of abandoning the exploratory drilling … as long as authority could be obtained and prospective sites remained to be tested…."[14]

Having found the Antelope Creek area unsuitable, focus shifted downstream. However, three studies near Elbow and Outlook (a site favoured by influential residents of Regina and Moose Jaw) proved this area to be unsuitable as well. At this point PFRA chief engineer G.L. MacKenzie approached Spence concerning tests at Coteau Creek. When Spence pointed out to MacKenzie that this was the third time that he had proposed a new region, MacKenzie replied, "That is all right so long as the river holds out."[15] Clearly, the engineers believed that somewhere along the river a suitable site would be found.

The Coteau site had certain advantages: less earth fill would be required; the higher elevation would permit gravity feeds from the resulting reservoir; and it was an ideal location for a power generating plant, since 53 percent of the population of the province would be within 125 miles and 69 percent within 150 miles. This point was important for recreational and water and power distribution purposes.

By mid-1947, then, after many years of investigation, PFRA officials finally settled on Coteau Creek as the site for the South Saskatchewan River Project. Choosing the site, however, was only one step in the long trail which had started nearly a century earlier and was destined to continue for more than a decade. As the technicians and administrators were soon to learn, there was more to building a dam of this size than moving earth and pouring concrete. It was now necessary to garner the political will to make the project a reality.

— THREE —

The Political Struggle Begins

The political struggles which began even before the final site was determined and which continued for the next decade were nearly as tortuous as the search for the site itself. But as tortuous as they were, a vocal group of supporters gradually coalesced to back Gardiner and the Saskatchewan government under T.C. Douglas. Collectively, these supporters gathered evidence which confirmed that the problems of the drought had not ended with the 1930s and that the country must look ahead to future droughts which would surely occur.

While those supporting the project approached the problem with arguments that differed in detail and subtlety, those arguments also had certain fundamental bases in common: all included a set of historical facts, current trends, and future predictions which those in authority — in this case, the federal government — could hardly ignore. The arguments centred on a set of major themes: the appalling impact of the drought; the subsequent need for relief funds from all levels of government; the population exodus and the realization that the problems of the region did not end with the 1930s;

and finally, that the answer to this recurring state of affairs lay in capturing the only visible source of water for irrigation, for urban and industrial supply, and for the production of a hydroelectric generating station. Less often stressed, but nonetheless important, were flood control, enhancement of recreational opportunities, and a particular theme — espoused repeatedly by Gardiner — that the federal government owed the region some special considerations because of the ill-advised settlement policies of the early years.

Among the advocates of the SSRP was a grassroots group formed in 1946 under the name of the Saskatchewan Rivers Development Association (SRDA). Its objectives were:

> to promote the conservation and utilization of the waters of the South Saskatchewan River for irrigation, power development and as a source of domestic water supply… Active memberships in the association consisted of cities, towns, rural municipalities, boards of trade and other organized bodies interested in the objective of the association.[1]

Initial SRDA membership fees ranged from $1 for associates to $500 for cities with a population over 10,000. Annual dues thereafter were to be determined by the executive but not to exceed the initial fees. The first meeting was attended by representatives from Regina, Saskatoon, Moose Jaw and eighteen rural municipalities.

A letter from the newly created body, dated May 8, 1946, listed Harold Pope, a Moose Jaw lawyer, as president and G. O'Shaunessy of the Moose Jaw Board of Trade as secretary. The letter urged rural municipalities which would benefit from the project to join the association. Notable among the statements in this letter was the following:

> The Honourable James G. Gardiner has assured us that the building of a dam on the South Saskatchewan River is already in the program of the Federal Government and this work will be undertaken as soon as the necessary engineering data has been secured in order to enable PFRA to choose the proper site for the construction of such a dam.[2]

It also included some preliminary observations, elaborating on its objective:

> irrigation … will mean that lands … of little value for wheat farming … will be brought under production and become very valuable and desirable properties … it is not the intention, of course, that good wheat land be used for this purpose… . The work of our association will not only be to secure the construction of the dam at the earliest possible time but in addition to organize irrigation districts … and then obtain industries which will process the products … from irrigated lands.[3]

Along with the SRDA, a number of pressure groups took up the call, including the Saskatchewan Farmers Union, the Saskatchewan School Trustees Association, a number of labour unions, the teachers federation, retail merchants groups, chambers of commerce, and associations of both rural and urban municipalities. The activities of these groups kept the South Saskatchewan River Project in high profile. But the prime minister of the day, Louis St. Laurent, preoccupied with the massive St. Lawrence Seaway project, was in no rush to divert public funds into the sparsely populated Prairies at the expense of more heavily populated regions of Ontario and Quebec.

The preparatory work of the PFRA continued despite St. Laurent's foot-dragging. By the late 1940s, according to a status report filed by L.B. Thomson, who had replaced Spence as PFRA director, the project was well advanced on many fronts.[4] The site had been established. A preliminary engineering report, tabled in the House of Commons by July 1947, included an approximate outline of the irrigable area. Plans were in place to feed the Qu'Appelle system. Two years of work had gone into the design of the dam. Site soil mechanics, drainage, seepage and climatological studies were well in hand. Results of soil surveys nearing completion revealed that more land was suitable for irrigation than first expected. A complete economic and land-use study was well underway. Agreements were being shaped between PFRA and the Saskatchewan Power Commission; an interim report of recreation aspects was in hand. The Prairie Provinces Water Board was working on apportionment of water between the three prairie provinces. And finally, a predevelopment farm was being readied for operation for the spring of 1950 on

120 acres of land sold to the federal Department of Agriculture by the town of Outlook for the sum of $5. All of this might have been comforting to those who were advocating the completion of the project had it not been for the fact that the federal government had not yet approved the project, and there was no agreement — if it were approved — concerning how much of the cost would fall to the province.

There is no doubt that Gardiner and Douglas were working together on the project, as their papers include a number of exchanges between the two which refer to both official and private meetings.[5] One of the main stumbling blocks to proceeding with the project, however, continued to be St.

View of the sign at the entrance of PFRA's pre-development farm for the South Saskatchewan River Project (c. 1947). Photo courtesy SAB — R-B8282.

Laurent, who repeatedly insisted that he would not approve it until he was certain that it would be of benefit to all of Canada. Gardiner, in an attempt to convince the prime minister that the SSRP would indeed benefit the nation, kept hammering away at this theme whenever possible — in discussions with Douglas, in Parliament, and sometimes in public. Some of these statements drew sharply worded rebukes in letters from the prime minister.

The Royal Commission

Eventually, St. Laurent proposed to Gardiner that the project's worth be tested through a study by a special committee, and a Royal Commission was struck on August 24, 1951 under the chairmanship of Dr. T.H. Hogg, with G.A. Gaherty, Dr. John A. Widtsoe, and Burton T. Richardson (secretary) as members. Their mandate was to determine

[w]hether the economic and social returns to the Canadian people on the investment in the proposed South Saskatchewan River Project ... would be commensurate with the cost thereof ... [and] [w]hether the said Project represent[ed] the most profitable and desirable use ... of the physical resources involved.[6]

During Commission hearings held in Outlook attended by 1,000 persons, not a single voice was raised in opposition to the undertaking. Nor was there any opposition at any of the other meetings in the province.[7] Submissions to the Outlook hearing and to hearings in Regina and Saskatoon from diverse groups — including farmers and labour organizations, teacher and trustee associations, boards of trade, urban and rural municipalities, and the province of Saskatchewan — supported the project. One such submission came from the Saskatchewan Rivers Development Association, which included the following statistics in its presentation to the Commission:

The rural municipality of Rudy lying adjacent to the town of Outlook is typical of the whole southern half of the proposed area.

1931-1950 — average wheat yield was 6.9 bu. per acre.

1931-1941 — a 10 year period ... less than 5 bu. per acre.

1941-1950 — 4 paying crops — 1939-42-43-44.

1931-1951 — relief or dried out bonus ... 17 years out of 20... .

Population: One of the worst results has been ... depopulation.

In 1925: farm pop. in area 31,000, in 1951, 16,300....

Education: ... In Outlook school unit :

1931	4,114 students
1951	1,600 students
1931	110 schools
1951	67 schools

... "Unless school authorities can be assured of a more reliable and dependable income then an adequate program of education cannot be expected in that area."[8]

Another submission from eighteen rural municipalities in the development region reflected a similar pattern, reporting that over the previous twenty years (1931-1951) the number of farmers in the ten townships of the Rosedale municipality had decreased by about 100 separate units, while the rural population in the same area had dropped from 1,789 in 1926 to 1,205 in 1941 to 881 in 1951. Rural population for all eighteen municipalities dropped from 31,672 in 1926 to 20,514 in 1946 to 18,297 in 1951. During that same period total population had increased from 70,282 in 1926 to 74,808 by 1946 and to 79,040 in 1951.[9] An examination of these figures, on balance, supports the contention of the SRDA that problems in the agricultural sector did not vanish with the end of the Dirty Thirties.

Submissions to the Royal Commission from Alberta and Manitoba, while not stating outright support, did nothing to detract from the project. Alberta outlined the benefits that would accrue and went on to make a plea for expanding the project into that province. The Manitoba submission included the complete texts of the apportion agreements signed by the three prairie provinces.

In October 1952, as it neared completion of the report, the commission summoned L.B. Thomson to Ottawa to discuss some of its findings. In essence, the views the commissioners presented to him were those which were to appear in the published report, even though Thomson challenged many of them on the spot. Despite Thomson's efforts, despite broadly based support for the project, and despite the impressive mass of information gathered by the commission members — the report was 274 pages along with a 149-page appendix of submissions (such as those by the SRDA, the eighteen rural municipalities, and numerous other agencies and organizations) — the report tabled on January 19, 1953, concluded

> that at present the economic returns to the Canadian people on the investment in the proposed South Saskatchewan River Project … are not commensurate with the cost thereof ….
>
> [and] that the available data, which are by no means complete, indicate that the said Project does not represent the most profitable and desirable use which can be made of the physical resources involved.[10]

Response to the Royal Commission Report

Not surprisingly, the report was met with hostility. Nor was the negative response to the commission's recommendations confined to the special interest groups who had defended and supported the project at the commission hearings. Both the province of Saskatchewan (publicly) and the federal minister of Agriculture (privately) attacked the findings.

The Saskatchewan response, published in a pamphlet, began:

> The tabling and publication of the report of the Royal Commission … has evoked a storm of protest in all parts of the nation. Despite the seemingly overwhelming economic, social and political evidence in favour of the project, the Commission has succeeded in producing an unfavorable report.[11]

The project, this pamphlet contended, had been consistently supported by the province and thus, the commission report was "a bitter disappointment to the people of Saskatchewan all of whom would benefit."[12] The Saskatchewan response challenged the cost estimates assumed by the commission, which were nearly a third higher than those of the PFRA, and dismissed the commission's estimates of benefits:

> The commission was [unrealistic] but surrounded its estimates with so many inconsistencies and qualifications that it is rather difficult to comment clearly.[13]

The Saskatchewan government quoted Rainer Schickele, Head of the Department of Agricultural Economics at North Dakota Agricultural College, concerning the commission's suggestion that land development programs were not justified in the face of threatening farm surpluses:

> Farm surpluses, except for a few special commodities during certain periods, are the result of demand rather than supply maladjustments and hence should be tackled primarily from the demand side. Moreover, erosion continues to sap productive capacity of agricultural land while the population increases.[14]

The pamphlet concluded:

> It remains for the government of Canada to assure the people of Saskatchewan and Canada that it is prepared to assume its responsibilities on the Project immediately. The Province of Saskatchewan has already renewed its original commitment with the full confidence that the project is feasible and crucial to the province and the nation.[15]

T.C. (Tommy) Douglas (1904-86), premier of Saskatchewan from 1944-61. Photo courtesy SAB — R-A5729-4.

The "original commitment" referred to in this pamphlet concerned discussions about provincial and federal financial responsibilities for the project between Gardiner and some members of the provincial government which were confirmed in a letter dated February 10, 1951 from the Saskatchewan premier, T.C. Douglas. Broadly stated (though many of the details were still to be negotiated), Saskatchewan would assume responsibility for the irrigation and power generation as well as a share of the added cost of the dam occasioned by the power element, while the federal government would cover the cost of the dam itself.

While the response of the Saskatchewan government was immediately made public, that of the federal government was more muted (it *was*, after all, the government's Royal Commission). Gardiner, however, was forthright in a 34-page secret report submitted to the federal Cabinet. In that report, he meticulously countered the points raised by the commissioners, frequently using their own arguments against them. He concluded by observing that the commission's findings were so flawed that they actually strengthened the case for the South Saskatchewan River Project:

> I have not dealt with paragraphs 3, 4-5, 6-7-8 and 9 because they exhibit a lack of knowledge of what is being done under PFRA, which indicates

that the commissioners were not possessed of sufficient knowledge to make their proposals worth while. ... In short I propose that we thank the commission for having strengthened our opinion that the South Saskatchewan Project should be proceeded with as soon as possible.[16]

Gardiner's letter to the prime minister himself concerning the commission report placed the South Saskatchewan River Project within the context of Gardiner's own experience:

> I became 21 the year before the province of Saskatchewan was formed. I have taken part in every provincial and federal election since. I have lived all these issues, and therefore probably place greater importance upon them than others do.[17]

Such a statement reflects an important difference between many advocates and opponents of the SSRP. Those living outside the affected region might have heard or read about conditions, and might have become more sympathetic as a result (as Mackenzie King obviously was in his talk with Spence), but those who had lived through the drought of the 1930s were scarred for life by the experience.

Beyond the Initial Responses

The unsatisfactory report of the Royal Commission did not, in fact, bring an end to the efforts to bring to reality the South Saskatchewan River Project. It is evident from the exchange of letters between Douglas and Gardiner that they continued to meet regularly, sometimes privately, working towards an agreement between the province and the government of Canada. By December 9, 1954, Gardiner and L.B. Thomson, Douglas and three of his ministers had come to substantial agreement on the terms. At this point, Gardiner decided to bring the prime minister up to date in a confidential letter. St. Laurent's response was a sharp rebuke:

> I feel that I should be quite frank in saying I am very much disturbed by this and pointing out at once some of my reasons for being so disturbed. … To sum up, I am afraid you have put us in the position where Saskatchewan Ministers can say that they were prepared to agree to everything you thought was reasonable and that there is no margin left for any real negotiations on any other basis. I cannot help but feel that this is not apt to help toward an early favorable decision.[18]

Although Gardiner replied to St. Laurent in a conciliatory tone, he did not relent in his efforts to muster support for the SSRP. Douglas, too, corresponded and set up meetings with St. Laurent following a provincial-federal conference. He occasionally took his case to the public, insisting that Saskatchewan was ready to share the cost as soon as the federal government agreed, and urging it to do so.

Meanwhile the Saskatchewan Rivers Development Association was not silent. On May 4, 1953, this organization had submitted a detailed plea to St. Laurent to go ahead with the project. It was accompanied by letters of support from the city of Regina, the Saskatchewan Farmers Union, the Saskatchewan Association of Rural Municipalities, a dozen rural municipalities, the Saskatchewan Wheat Pool, the Saskatchewan Board of Trade, and the Saskatchewan Urban Municipalities Association. Yet, despite this pressure, St. Laurent remained adamant that he was not yet convinced that the project was in the best interest of Canada as a whole, and that he would make no move on it until he had concluded that it was.

Prior to the federal election of 1957, Gardiner again put great pressure on the prime minister to approve the project as part of the platform. When St. Laurent demurred on the basis that he did not want it to become a political issue, Gardiner disagreed, insisting that

> all political parties and most individuals [favor the project] … [T]he only way it can be political is for the government to refuse to go along with all the others. It could become a real issue in Saskatchewan overshadowing all others.[19]

Once the election had been called, St. Laurent could no longer dodge questions. During a campaign swing through Saskatchewan, a question was raised about the South Saskatchewan River Project. He responded sharply:

> There has been no decision. I'm sure that this project offers many benefits but I'm not prepared to give a definite answer until I can tell Parliament that I'm certain the nation would get more out of it than it would put into it.[20]

Douglas, too, was still pushing for a federal commitment. In a letter to St. Laurent dated April 29, 1957, he expressed "deep disappointment" that the prime minister had not made "an affirmative decision" on the project.[21] Douglas suggested another meeting with the prime minister as soon as the election was over. This suggestion, of course, was academic. When the dust cleared after the election, the Liberals were out of power, St. Laurent was no longer prime minister, and John G. Diefenbaker was poised to fulfill his promise that the SSRP would go ahead once he was elected. This turned out to be a little complicated in that Diefenbaker was sitting with a minority government and struggling to keep it afloat. However, in 1958 Diefenbaker took his case to the people and rolled to victory with a huge majority, setting the stage for concrete action on the SSRP.

— FOUR —

"A Dam Site Surer and a Dam Site Sooner"

In the tense political climate in the months prior to the federal election of 1958, Prime Minister John G. Diefenbaker began to show particular interest in the South Saskatchewan River Project. In Diefenbaker's papers there is a note to an aide, ordering him to see if evidence could be found proving that Jimmy Gardiner — Diefenbaker's principal Liberal opponent in the struggle for Saskatchewan votes — had once wavered in his support for the project. To Diefenbaker's disappointment, the reply was negative.[1] Also among these papers are sundry notes on what appear to be scraps of hotel stationery, with phrases such as "The Liberals won't give a dam but the PCs will" and "The Liberals didn't think Saskatchewan was worth a dam," followed by a series of revisions concluding with "It will be a dam site surer and a dam site sooner if you re-elect John Diefenbaker," which appeared as the title of a brochure distributed in Saskatchewan during the campaign.[2]

Manoeuvring Toward a Dam Agreement

And sooner it certainly was. Diefenbaker's Progressive Conservatives were swept back into power with an overwhelming majority, and all that stood between federal-provincial agreement on the project was a bit of political manoeuvring. After all, Diefenbaker's campaign in Saskatchewan was based on the dam issue and he was on record as favouring the SSRP as early as 1949,[3] so the resistance at the federal level exhibited by St. Laurent simply no longer existed. The position of the Saskatchewan government had not changed, of course, and correspondence between Diefenbaker and Saskatchewan premier T.C. Douglas, and their public statements on the topic, indicate that the two men remained in fundamental agreement about the project.

John G. Diefenbaker (1895-1979), thirteenth prime minister; his 1958 campaign in Saskatchewan focused on the dam. Photo courtesy SAB — R-A28141.

One area still under negotiation at the time of the 1958 federal election was Douglas's request that Saskatchewan's commitment be a fixed sum rather than a percentage of the total costs. Then, a month before the 1958 election, Douglas wrote Diefenbaker with an additional request: that the federal government provide the province with an interest-free loan to help cover Saskatchewan's share of the costs.[4] On the day following the election Douglas sent Diefenbaker a telegram congratulating him on his victory, and added that "Legislation on South Saskatchewan River dam [is] now before the legislature and a reply to my letter of March 4 would greatly facilitate the passage."[5] Douglas Harkness, Diefenbaker's minister of Agriculture, replied on May 15, stating: "The Dominion Government does not consider that the costs … would be of such a magnitude as to impose any undue difficulty on the Government of Saskatchewan in financing these costs … spread over a considerable period of time."[6]

Douglas pressed his argument again in letters to Harkness and Diefenbaker dated May 21 and June 12, but received a negative response on both occasions.[7] Frustrated, Douglas issued a press release on July 2, in which he accused Diefenbaker of "rank discrimination against Saskatchewan" for failing to come up with the loan, but declared he would sign the agreement anyway.[8] Diefenbaker suspected Douglas of trying to make political mileage out of the situation, and a hand-written note on a copy of the press release in Diefenbaker's papers reads: "Premier generating some pre-election ????"[9]

Suspicions about gaining political mileage from the project also ran the other way. T.J. Bentley, a longtime member of Douglas's cabinet, warned the premier that Diefenbaker stood to gain full credit for the SSRP:

many of the people in the Southwest Corner of the province are under the impression that when the dam is built it will be mostly at federal expense by virtue of dear old John. Hence there is an inclination to praise John from whom this blessing flows … [I suggest] that when final agreements are drawn up a clear-cut statement be made in every weekly newspaper and every other media … to acquaint people [with details of the roles played by the various political parties, and a division of the costs].[10]

Bentley's concerns were not unfounded. The SSRP did indeed come to be closely associated with the

Below: Prime Minister Diefenbaker throws the switch to set off a charge of dynamite and declare the South Saskatchewan River Project officially open in May 1959.
Photo courtesy SAB — R-A14084.

Right: Premier T.C. Douglas poses atop an earth-moving machine at the official inauguration of construction, May 1959.
Photo courtesy SAB — R-B12762.

government of John Diefenbaker. Ironically, however, the terms of the federal-provincial agreement were essentially those which had been negotiated between Jimmy Gardiner and T.C. Douglas prior to the Liberal defeat in the 1957 federal election. They called for the federal government to accept responsibility for construction of the two dams required to create the reservoir, while the province would cover the costs of the power-generating plant, irrigation works, and 25 percent of the cost of the main dam. And while Douglas lost his battle to secure a loan from the federal government, he did succeed in his quest to have Saskatchewan's share fixed. In the final agreement, signed on July 25, 1958, Saskatchewan's share of the costs of the dam was fixed at 25 percent, but in the case of cost over-runs would not exceed $25 million.

The signing was met with jubilation by the PFRA staff and their counterparts in the federal Department of Agriculture. According to J. Gordon Watson, who was assistant chief engineer with PFRA at the time, on the day following the signing of the agreement, a telegram arrived in PFRA headquarters from the deputy minister of Agriculture which read: "Agreement signed. What are you waiting for?" Not to be outdone, the PFRA staff immediately got down to business: the first tenders were called for less than a week later, contracts were awarded within a month, and equipment was on the site by early September. By the end of 1958, seven contracts valued at more than $5 million had been let.

The start of work on the project did not bring an end to the political jockeying. Some eight months after the first ground was broken at the dam site, on May 27, 1959, the project was officially opened when 750 pounds of dynamite were triggered by John Diefenbaker. Organizers of the event had thought that T.C. Douglas would be asked to share in the ceremonial blast, and arranged for the trigger mechanism to be equipped with a handle long enough to accommodate both men. However, when the time came, Douglas was shuffled aside and Diefenbaker triggered the blast alone.[11] That night, during the dinner ceremonies that followed the opening, another "oversight" occurred. Diefenbaker spoke glowingly of how the SSRP had united Saskatchewan politicians from across the political spectrum. Yet, though he was present at the dinner, Jimmy Gardiner, who had devoted so much time and effort to the project, was not included among the speakers. In an editorial, the Rosetown *Eagle* took organizers to task for this slight to Gardiner, but otherwise the omission appears to have escaped media notice.

Despite the political manoeuvrings, the second largest public works project in Canadian history was officially underway. Although there were still some contentious issues, for the moment morale was high and a spirit of euphoria surrounded the project. Unfortunately, it was not to last.

Crowds gather for the official opening of the South Saskatchewan River Project, May 1959. Photo courtesy SAB — R-A14084 (1).

— FIVE —

"Irrigate or Migrate"

While there were to be five principal components to the South Saskatchewan River Project — irrigation, hydroelectric power, flood control, recreation, and urban and industrial water supply — to a region still traumatized by the devastating drought of the 1930s, the most important aspect of the project was clearly the potential of irrigation to "drought-proof" the farm lands which had been reduced to fruitless desert a generation earlier. Ironically, it was this focus on irrigation that was to lead to serious disagreements about the nature and development of the SSRP. Among the provisions of the agreement between the two governments was a provincial commitment to have facilities in place to irrigate 50,000 acres within a year of the time the reservoir was filled. In order to do so, the government would have to enlist the cooperation of farmers in the area surrounding the dam. That cooperation was not, however, to be assumed.

The minutes of a cabinet committee meeting early in 1959 indicate that the provincial government looked to experience with irrigation projects in Alberta for indications of how farmers would respond to such projects. Based on experience in Alberta, it was, in fact, apparent that farmers were typically unable to pay any sizable portion of the capital cost of an irrigation development and that, where there was an alternative in dry land farming, farmers would not generally use irrigation works, unless measures were used that required them to do so. The measures decided upon were as follows: first, a water tax was imposed on all lands deemed to be irrigable (whether the water was used or not); and second, the government offered to buy the land of those not wishing to irrigate. Such measures were immediately seen by farmers as threatening and dictatorial. Irritated farmers quickly coined the phrase "Irrigate or Migrate."

Resisting Irrigation: the Irrigation Investigation Group

One such group of farmers north of Broderick eyed the switch to irrigation with apprehension, and chats along "coffee row" became more formal with the establishment of the Irrigation Investigation Group (IIG) at a meeting on the farm of the Larson brothers on November 5, 1958. Their objective was to "investigate all situations which will arise from the South Saskatchewan Irrigation Project with a view in mind of protecting the rights of ownership and control by the resident farmers."[1]

In order to address its mandate, the group sought legal advice, made inspection tours of irrigation projects in Alberta, and interviewed knowledgeable individuals who cast shadows over the sunny expectations of irrigation. The IIG then set out to apprise provincial authorities of the irritation and concerns of the approximately 100 farmers who made up its membership. It proposed remedies through letters, briefs, press releases and face-to-face meetings with government.

The IIG revelled in the role of victim, claiming in a newspaper interview that "government treatment of dryland farmers in the area was the worst violation of the Bill of Rights in the World today."[2] One IIG brief to government quoted Professor H. Van Vliet, head of the University of Saskatchewan Department of Farm Management:

What I chiefly fear is that the original settler in such a high cost project, will be saddled with an excessive load of development costs, whereby he will become a guinea pig of the process and carry too much of the burden of establishing the project for future generations.[3]

The IIG emphasized that its members were not opposed to irrigation, but instead objected to the pressure tactics being employed by the government. Of particular concern to farmers in the area was their seeming inability to get the information they needed to help them determine whether a switch to irrigation would be profitable. Farmers worried about what they saw as four serious drawbacks to irrigation: high cost of development, high cost of production, lack of markets, and low returns on agricultural products. The apparent reluctance of the government to deal with their concerns only raised the level of suspicion.

Ultimately, many farmers feared that they would somehow lose a measure of their independence if they acceded to the government's pressure to adopt irrigation. Dawson Young, a PFRA surveyor at the time who had grown up in the Broderick area, and whose father was a member of the IIG, recalls hearing a farmer state: "I didn't spend my life on the farm all these years to wind up as a coolie mucking around up to my knees in mud." Other farmers echoed this sentiment. That this vision of irrigation farming did not quite square with reality was of little consequence — quite simply, this was how many farmers felt.

The IIG, supported by the local branch of the Saskatchewan Farmers Union, offered the following proposals (summarized here) which it felt would allay the fears of its membership:

1. That farmers wishing to continue dryland farming be exempt from paying the water tax on undeveloped land.
2. That the government keep expanding irrigation farming on a volunteer basis. The present compulsory policy is inadequate for the following reasons: a) it does not take into account existing adverse economic conditions facing agriculture; b) it does not take into account the age of

dryland farmers in the area; c) it does not recognize the varying degrees of ability to learn irrigation farming; d) more outside interest would be shown to purchase private land — people not only fear but frown on government compulsion.

3. That government should purchase, at fair value, the farm of any farmer who develops land for irrigation and decides by reason of disability or other legitimate reasons not to continue.

4. That farmers who are forced to sell land be permitted to go before a board of arbitration to seek just settlement.

5. That any legal expense accruing to the farmer from expropriation be paid by the government. Present expropriation laws are unfair.

6. That farmers who cannot renew crown land leases for next year be permitted to use present grain storage until next July 31, and, in some cases, be permitted to store machinery on the property until they have had time to make other arrangements.

7. That government cover costs of levelling all land determined to be irrigable and recover this cost by the farmer operating the land at a yearly rate of assessment spread over a 40-year period, such payments to be interest free.

8. That the government arrange for interest-free loans for development of land for irrigation.

9. That, in addition to buying the farms of those not wishing to irrigate, the government should help with resettlement costs.

10. That the water tax be waived for the first three years of irrigation development because benefits during the break-in period would be meager. The tax should then be introduced on a gradual scale over 15 years and then not exceed $2.50 per acre.

The IIG also suggested that the government establish a marketing board to purchase specialty crops, construct canning factories and other food processing plants, and agree to purchase all produce at standard market prices.

At the centre of this debate were some fundamental misunderstandings, and some puzzling omissions of meaningful information exchange. An *Act of the Department of Agriculture,* passed in 1962 to set forth a framework under which the government could proceed with establishment of an irrigation system, provided for the government's right to expropriate land for canals, distribution works, and reservoirs needed to deliver the service. Some farmers interpreted this to mean that their farms could be expropriated if they did not irrigate, although that was not the intention. The *Act* also established the mechanism for the creation of "irrigation districts" for those wanting to irrigate. These organizations could be created only after a two-thirds majority vote of farmers in the area.

Surveys — like this one conducted near Elbow c. 1947 — continued despite protests from some local farmers. Photo courtesy SAB — R-B8285.

"Surveys Prohibited"

Unfortunately, the provincial government was working under a deadline. In order to meets its obligations under the terms of the federal-provincial agreement, it had to have 50,000 acres of land ready for the irrigation project. To accomplish this, it was necessary to conduct extensive exploratory work in advance of the creation of the irrigation districts. This involved determining the suitability of soil for irrigation, land levels, drainage patterns, and suitable water storage sites. Consequently, survey crews were obliged to enter farm lands in the region in which they were working.

Members of the IIG interpreted this "invasion" of their property as indicating that the government had predetermined that their farms would be committed to irrigation. They complained vociferously that the *Act* of 1962 had promised a vote which they had been denied, and that the government had thus broken its own law.

The IIG and the government remained at loggerheads for almost four years. Finally, frustrated farmers decided to try some new tactics. They spent $42 for 1,000 "Surveys Prohibited" signs which the members then posted on their land. As well, a letter was sent to the minister of Agriculture, demanding that all surveyors be withdrawn immediately. Shortly thereafter, a group of farmers blocked the entrance to one farm, and forced the surveyors to turn back.

This incident triggered a persistent — but unfounded — rumour that the police intervened to escort surveyors onto the land, to the accompanying catcalls of "police state." Arlo Larson, an IIG member who was himself involved in this confrontation, said that the situation never got out of hand. The surveyors, faced by the group of farmers, simply shouldered their instruments and departed. A few days later the matter was resolved when the police informed the farmers of the legalities involved. This was confirmed in the minutes of an IIG meeting on November 9, 1965:

> Sergeant Simpson, RCMP, addressed the group on the action taken by the group pertaining to the removal of surveyors from the land. He suggested that we could be charged with assault for telling the surveyors to leave the land because by law they are rightfully there.[4]

A letter from the minister of Agriculture, which confirmed the police position, was tabled at the same meeting. Larson said that this put an end to the obstructionist tactics, adding "we weren't lawbreakers."

Despite the bad feelings generated up to this point by the government's tactics, officials involved in the project still spoke publicly about the need for "a certain amount of compulsion" to get dryland farmers to switch to irrigation. According to one newspaper account, an on-site engineering supervisor said this compulsion would take the form of "charges for irrigation at an anticipated rate of $4.50 per acre to be charged against the land whether or not the farmer irrigated."[5] This policy remained a constant irritant until 1977, when the government finally agreed to pay the amount due from this tax on unirrigated land in the form of a grant to the irrigation district, rather than holding the landowner responsible.

From Loggerheads to Dialogue

On April 7, 1966, the government passed *An Act to Provide for the Establishment and Development of the South Saskatchewan River Irrigation Project.* This *Act* helped resolve some of the difficulties faced by potential irrigators. One provision of this *Act* established the principle of government grants for land preparation for those farmers wishing to irrigate, thus partially replacing the concept of compulsion with one of enticement.

On June 17, 1967, just prior to the official opening of the dam, details of the support plan were jointly announced by the provincial minister of Agriculture, D.T. McFarlane, and the federal minister of Forestry and Rural Development, Maurice Sauvé. Sauvé spoke on behalf of the *Agriculture and Rural Development Act* (ARDA), a joint federal-provincial agency which would bear the costs of the land preparation grants. The amount of these grants was set at one-third of the development cost after deduction of the first $1,000, to a maximum of $35 per developed acre. The funds would be available to both individual installations or group enterprises. The minimum size for installations was set at 10 acres to a maximum size of 100 acres, with maximum grants of $3,000 per farm. In addition to these funds, the plan included free technical advice on management of irrigation and payment of interest charges on money borrowed to make the change.

In lieu of development grants, farmers would be eligible for loans on which the interest would be waived for seven years if the loan was taken out in the first year that water became available. For each year of delay following the first year, the length of time of waived interest would be reduced by one year.

The South Saskatchewan River Irrigation Project Advisory Committee

Government authorities made another move toward more meaningful dialogue with farmers by creating the South Saskatchewan River Irrigation Project Advisory Committee; its mandate was

> to recommend to the government measures which, in their opinion, would assist in the conversion of the area from dryland to irrigation farming, and in the solving of problems faced by farmers in the course of the development of the project and conversion of the area to irrigation farming."[6]

The Committee was chaired by J.A. Brown, Agricultural Economics Department, University of Saskatchewan, and included an economist from the provincial Department of Agriculture, and three farmers, one of whom, Arlo Larson, had been an active voice in the IIG. Thus a bridge was built between the government and one of its most vocal critics.

Saskatchewan River Development Association speakers explain the project with the help of illustrations at this July 1958 meeting overlooking the dam site. Information meetings such as this helped to create dialogue instead of resistance. Photo courtesy SAB — R-B12742.

Cover of a pamphlet promoting the benefits of irrigation farming. Photo courtesy SAB — R-B10779.

The Committee moved quickly to reduce tensions in the area. It held twelve regular meetings in the eighteen months after its creation, toured the SSRP and several irrigation projects in Alberta, initiated several research projects, and submitted preliminary resolutions to the government of Saskatchewan.

In its first report, the Committee outlined its role as follows:

1. To determine the nature and extent of problems in the area and refer them to the minister;

2. To consider needs and wishes of the farmers in the area, those wishing to irrigate and those not wishing to irrigate to sell affected land, and to put forward suitable policy suggestions accordingly;

3. Help determine areas of needed research, whether for purposes of the Committee or broader purposes;

4. Assist in deciding upon information and extension services required in the area and;

5. Work toward desirable development of the area as a whole, as well as of individual farms.[7]

The report examined land-purchase policies, land values, subsidies for development, water rates, loans to farmers, leasing arrangements and general impacts of switching to irrigation. It concluded there would be potential markets for fodder from dairy farmers and beef herdsmen alike, examined the possibility of pea production, and initiated a more extensive study of this crop to determine its feasibility, along with the possible production of alfalfa meal.

The committee's field trips to Alberta were useful in that they allowed for some fairly reliable estimates of expected yields on which to base projections of benefits in Saskatchewan. It was also noted that production on irrigated fields would improve fairly dramatically during the first three years but would level off as farmers gained more experience after the third year. Thus farmers were forewarned about what they might expect. Among the secondary enterprises, the Committee felt there would be a good potential in cow-calf operations, along with feedlot operations, hogs, forage production, alfalfa crops, and leafcutter bees.

The report also stressed the need for high-quality construction and land development standards in order to minimize canal and side ditch seepage, which would aggravate the ever-present potential problem of salinity damage. It recommended the need for an extension program to introduce dryland farmers into the intricacies of irrigated operations, emphasizing that such services be offered as a separate mission detached from the regular agricultural representative's duties because of its specialized nature.

On the basis of a detailed economic comparison of two dryland operations and two irrigated operations, the Committee concluded that

> if major markets for grain were not a problem, an optimistic view could be taken of the economic returns from irrigated farming. With quota restrictions, these economic returns would be dependent in large part upon individual initiative in successfully growing non-quota crops and making adjustment through diversification.[8]

This conclusion underscored the oft-repeated call for greater diversity upon which more stable operations could be built.

The report outlined certain drawbacks to the introduction of irrigation farming. There would be some disruption to the farm communities since some farmers were too young to retire but too old to start over on irrigation farms. As well, long-established dryland farms would be broken up. The report added, however, that after irrigation was established, farm life in the area would improve "because of such things as improved roads, more social services and more people to support schools, hospitals and other community projects."[9]

The Committee revisited the question of compensation for land being acquired by the government from those who did not wish to participate in the irrigation program:

> There is widespread opinion that land prices and the present land purchase policy are not equitable among different sellers. For example, parcels of high quality dry land without improvements are valued too low by present formulas relative to inferior lands with improvements. To quite an extent it appears the improvements have been used as a vehicle for providing compensation for "disruption." Potential for irrigability has resulted in further distortion of prices relative to dry land values.[10]

To rectify this situation the Committee suggested:

> (a) that a schedule of purchase prices be established to conform with market prices for similar land in adjacent areas;
>
> (b) that irrigation allowances be discontinued; and
>
> (c) that disruption allowances be paid. Such allowances should be clearly identified apart from land prices and should not become part of the resale price of the land.
>
> The committee considers that all three of the above provisions are required in a new land purchase policy to adequately compensate owners who do not wish to irrigate. If such a policy is not adopted exemption from water tax for selected classes of operators should be considered.[11]

The report also suggested that those developing farms for irrigation enter into an agreement with the government, whereby the government would agree to buy out the farm and all improvements at a price determined at the time of the contract in the event that, through disability or other legitimate reason, the farmer was unable to continue the operation.

Another protection for the farmers was embodied in the suggestion that land reassessment by rural municipalities, based on the assumption that the irrigated operator would have an increased ability to pay, be delayed due to the fact that in the early years of development start-up costs and techniques would have a negative impact on returns. The Committee suggested a 6 percent ceiling on interest rates, the establishment of a government-operated fodder reserve to reduce marketing difficulties in fodder crops, extensive research into alternative lines of production, the use of sprinkler systems, and the creation of secondary industries. In order to encourage ventures into more experimental crops, the Committee recommended that a policy be established to provide price or income support for these experimental ventures. It was further suggested that a fund be established to encourage an expansion of livestock ventures.

In the years that followed, all of the Committee's suggestions were addressed, with the exception of the matter of assessment of irrigated land, which still had not been addressed in 1996. In particular, some of the cost-sharing methods discussed were covered by the Subsidary Agreement on Irrigation Based Economic Development (SIBED) and the Partnership Agreement on Water Based Economic Development (PAWBED).

Negotiation, not Expropriation

Unlike the animosity which greeted the government surveyors, the PFRA crews working in the area established a friendly rapport with local farmers. According to their supervisor, Dawson Young, the crews were even being treated to freshly baked pie by farm wives on whose fields they were working.

The PFRA surveyors' work was every bit as invasive as that of the government surveyors in the Broderick area. Indeed, it was even more so, since the PFRA's mission was the prelude to these farmers giving up lands they owned or leased to make way for the creation of the reservoir. Acquisition of these properties fell under PFRA jurisdiction as part of the federal agreement to create the reservoir. This involved establishing the boundaries (anticipated level of the waterline plus a reasonable margin of error), negotiating purchase of owned land and cancellation of leases held by farmers and ranchers on Crown land within these boundaries.

Farmer acceptance of these procedures was based partly on the fact that the mission was clearly stated and understood by the farmers as an essential part of the project, and while farmers would have to give up land they were not required to spend any money on development. In fact, the land that was given up was not especially valuable. According to a May 1960 article in the *Engineering Journal*, only 5,700 acres out of 109,600 acres in the floodplain were under cultivation. Bob Tullis, a Lucky Lake area farmer, lost two quarter sections which he said were marginal: as pasture land they could not sustain more than four or five head of cattle per quarter. Tullis considered prices fair at the time.

Another factor which eased the situation in the area under the PFRA's jurisdiction was the esteem in which it was held by a significant segment of the population throughout the prairie region. J. Gordon Watson, one-time director of the PFRA, remembers that Ross Thatcher, when he was premier of the province, observed that he had never seen a public institution which had developed the good will of the public to such an extent as had the PFRA. This, Watson felt, was due, in part, to the fact that PFRA had never been accused of "bullying" the people it worked for. Watson added that "all the directors of the organization insisted that staff keep in mind that they were the servants of the farmers and rural municipalities and they should be always tuned to their needs."

Perhaps this is why, according to PFRA files, the acquisition of land in the floodplain progressed smoothly. In response to a letter from a member of the Geography and Planning Department at the University of Waterloo, requesting information "on the effects of expropriation on people who have been displaced by construction of the public project," C.J. Paterson, coordinator of land acquisition for the SSRP, replied:

> It was necessary to acquire some 148,000 acres for right of way of which 58,000 acres was deeded land. To acquire the deeded land involved the completion of 241 deals. Two hundred and forty

of these were settled by negotiation and only in one case was expropriation necessary to acquire the property.[12]

That nearly every transaction was conducted through negotiation rather than expropriation is hardly surprising when one considers the respect and consideration that PFRA officials evidently showed to farmers with whom they dealt.

In one instance, A.S. Ringheim, a senior engineer, came upon damage to a fence and some crop during an inspection tour. In a letter to the administration he noted that the farmer in question had not complained. Nevertheless, Ringheim suggested that some compensation should be made for this damage, either as a lump sum or an added bonus when purchase of the property was negotiated.

In another case, Harold Horner, deputy minister of Agriculture, made a plea for special consideration for the plight of an aging woman whose husband had recently died. She was attempting to run the farm on her own and held some provincial Crown land on lease, which had been turned over to the federal government to expedite the creation of the reservoir. Normal procedure was to simply cancel such leases as their renewal dates came up. Horner suggested a delay in this case so as not to place additional hardship upon the widow; PFRA complied.

A Grave Situation

In the process of purchasing land and cancelling leases, PFRA arranged to have buildings moved and paid farmers for the cost of fences and other improvements on Crown land. Not all of these transactions were without incident. One of the most delicate transactions involved the Stone family. The father, Per Sten (whose name was later Anglicized to "Stone"), had entered the area from Minnesota in 1906 and died two years later. He was buried in the farm yard, which was located near the east abutment of the dam. Thus, in addition to the issue of acquiring the land, PFRA had to deal with the question of Per Sten's grave. The family finally agreed to have the grave moved. One of the grandsons, Gerald Stone, commended the government for the reverence and dignity with which it

handled the situation. A hearse was brought in to remove the remains and the ceremony was attended by a number of dignitaries and some family members. It was an emotional experience for family members, and an awkward silence hung over the gathering as the hearse pulled away. Then the tension was broken when one family member observed: "Gee, that's the first car ride the old man ever had."

For all the human melodrama involved with the acquisition of land, the political manoeuvrings, the heated debates, dedicated studies and legal reports, there was another, more spectacular face to the SSRP. Thousands of workers, at the controls of huge machines in round-the-clock shifts, were having an enormous impact on the landscape and the people who lived there, as work proceeded apace on the second-largest public works project in Canadian history.

— SIX —

A New Face for a Storied Stream

Many of the drowsy towns and villages along the South Saskatchewan awoke with a start at the signing of the agreement that would reshape the stream that flowed through their neighborhoods. They awoke, as Harold Longman of the Regina *Leader-Post* reported in 1958, "to find what once seemed hopeless dreams of progress now within their grasp." [1]

The anticipated long-term effect of the South Saskatchewan River Project has already been discussed in terms of the irrigation, power, and recreation to be provided by the dam itself. The shorter-term, yet still significant, effect was the influx of men and machinery on these drowsy towns and villages during the construction of the dam itself. Referring to the town of Outlook, Longman noted:

> Sales of town property have been heavy since the announcement … many new buildings are already under construction and permits let for many more.
>
> [These include] a large shopping centre, housing under one roof, stores, offices and a restaurant…

Outlook New Holdings Ltd. also proposes to build a large motor hotel and a pre-fabricated homes development.

Presently under construction are three service stations, a lumber yard, and a clothing store…. Also in the offing are two more motels, an electrical shop, paint and glass store, and a new restaurant.[2]

Longman reported that Loreburn and Broderick were experiencing similar activity, although on a smaller scale (Loreburn's population was about 200 compared to Outlook's which was nearly 1,000). Elbow was also viewed as one of the villages which stood to gain by the development.

Not every community in the area, however, experienced this kind of growth. Conrad Romuld reported in *The Western Producer* in May 1964 that, although the population of Dunblane had more than tripled, it had not experienced "the degree of commercial expansion that the population increase would lead one to expect."[3] Dawson Young, a survey chief with PFRA, lived in Dunblane at the time. To begin with, he dwelt in one room of the general store, which the proprietor had fashioned into a make-shift hotel. Each of the rooms was heated with a space heater fired by wood and coal. Young explained that when coming off the job, he was faced with hauling fuel from the shed at the rear of the establishment (room service of any kind was left to occupant rather than the proprietor). While the room was heating up he would sit in the coffee shop. Young said there were pipes running in every direction to take the smoke from these heating units. Later he hauled a trailer onto one of the village's two trailer parks and this was a typical way of coping with the need for accommodation for the increased population.

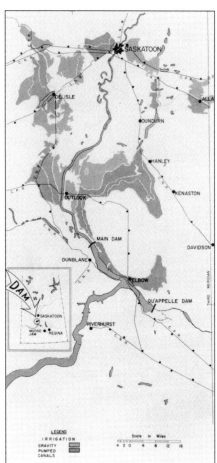

This map — entitled "South Saskatchewan River Development Project Irrigable Lands" — shows areas suitable for gravity irrigation and pumped irrigation and the location of canals. Photo courtesy SAB — R-A16414.

Some area farmers whose lands had been acquired began to move buildings into the village for use as either temporary or permanent residences. One resulting difficulty, of course, was that these were sometimes rather makeshift arrangements. The town fathers had to set rules on what could be built where, which gave rise to some acrimony, according to Len Bartzen who was mayor at the time.

Such caution on the part of town administration was also evident elsewhere, as Longman's article confirms. He reported:

> The thing that strikes you about Outlook is the fact that its optimism is tempered by good sense. In short there is no "boom town" talk here.
>
> "We want a steady permanent growth, not a sudden boom," says Coun. G.J. Brack, chairman of the town's busy property committee, "we don't want fly-by-night businesses."
>
> "We will not countenance speculation," says Mayor J.C. Carter, who at 76 is sitting in the mayor's chair for the third time. Tall, straight and active, Mr. Carter was the district's first homesteader coming here in 1903.
>
> "And we do not want any matchstick buildings." To prevent this, Mayor Carter explains that the town has recently been zoned, a building permit system instituted, and rigid code for builders laid down.[4]

In Outlook, the "steady permanent growth" that Brack spoke of was being achieved, evident in the growth of schools and health-care facilities. Longman's report continues:

> Larger school unit officials have bought most of three town blocks on which it is hoped to build, maybe next year, a large composite high school. A four room addition … is definitely planned at any rate.
>
> Lutheran College … is to build an $85,000 auditorium, an old folks home is on the drawing boards, two trailer courts are planned and an addition to Outlook's modern 20-bed hospital is mooted.[5]

The Dunblane school also had to cope with more students, but, again, the response was to make do with the available facilities, rather than building. In 1928, when the village had been established as a railway centre, the citizens had built a fine four-room red brick school. But from 1932 onward, as the effects of the Depression began to be felt, only three of the rooms were in use. Within months of the beginning of construction on the dam, however, the fourth room was once more pressed into service. Later, according to Patricia Stavenjord, a teacher at the time, the basement of the school was also turned into classrooms and the basement of the United Church was taken over to handle the overflow.

However, as Dawson Young explained, most of the people in Dunblane at the time doubted that the boom would be permanent. Although Andrew Romuld, farmer *cum* gasoline supplier, had two tank trucks going around the clock to supply the fleet of vehicles working on the dam, he was sanguine: when work on the dam was finished, his business would be too. The population of Dunblane reached a peak of 400, but dropped to 40 within months of the end of construction. Today, one cannot buy so much as a cup of coffee there.

The Work and the Workers

Three years after Harold Longman wrote of the anticipated boom in Outlook and other communities, he revisited the site and reported thus:

Men and machinery begin work at the dam site (c. 1959-60). Photo courtesy SAB — R-B12779.

Workers came from across Canada, from across the ocean, and from the communities which surrounded the dam site. Photo courtesy SAB — R-B12780 (3).

From a vantage point on the banks of the sluggish South Saskatchewan River Thursday I saw a marvel in the making.

Just three years ago I stood on this same spot when the South Saskatchewan River dam project that is going to harness this mighty and storied stream was still just a lot of paper plans.

I stood then on a hillside surrounded only by dry grass, stunted trees, a few cattle and silence.

Thursday I found the valley transformed. I stood surrounded by hundreds of scurrying machines, dust, noise and visible evidence of man's engineering prowess.

Millions of tons of earth have been piled into a great barrier that will eventually block the river and turn its strength to man's betterment.[6]

What Longman describes above in visual terms can also be seen in economic terms and in personal terms. A report of the South Saskatchewan River Project Development Commission, tabled in the legislature in March 1961, observed that by the end of 1960, $8 million had been spent in the province for materials, equipment and servicing for the dam's construction. By the end of 1960, workers on the dam had received nearly $250,000 in wages. The Commission estimated that by the time the dam was scheduled to be completed in 1968, this figure would stand at $17,000,000. The number of workers employed over this period would vary from less than 100 to a peak of about 1,300 in the summer of 1963.[7] The project drew heavily on the local communities for labour, but there was a considerable turnover since many of the employees were young farmers who left the dam to return to their farms during seeding and harvest.

In personal terms, however, the machines Longman saw scurrying about were being driven by *men* — many of them local, but many not. As Conrad Romuld noted, there was a definite international flavour to Dunblane at the time:

An aerial view of the construction headquarters and its surrounding village. Photo courtesy SAB — R-B4474(9).

> And they [the workers] are from everywhere. A few grew up within earshot of the din that never ends. A fifth of them manage to live at home and commute 10, 20 or 30 miles to work each day. But there's an engineer from Glasgow, another from Norway, a baker from Edinburgh, a laborer from Portugal. With them, into the general area, have come another 300 workers to man the gas pumps, the stores and the beer parlors where in some instances business is better than brisk.[8]

Members of the construction crews who were not hired locally were housed in "gaunt metal-sheathed barracks which [did] not look any more than barely comfortable even by austere Prairie standards."[9] These men were provided with hearty meals, seventeen times a day to meet the demand of the shifts even though the dining room looked, like the sleeping quarters, much on the rough and ready side.[10]

Meanwhile, over at the PFRA headquarters site, a surrounding village had been created, in which the amenities were far more upscale. In all, the compound consisted of an administration building, a staff house, an assembly hall, assorted garages and laboratory buildings, 36 single-family houses and two duplexes.[11] According to some of the inhabitants of these dwellings, they were most adequate, being constructed of frame or concrete block.

Sharon Baldwin, a young housewife and mother on the site stated that PFRA appeared to place a great deal of emphasis on the need to keep the people housed there happy. Although she had no first-hand experience of life in other camps, some of her neighbours did, and said the atmosphere and amenities were much better there than in other camps in which they had lived. The site was serviced with sewer, water, sidewalks and roads. As well, there was an ambulance and a fire truck in the complex.

The Assembly Hall in the camp was put to good use, with social events being held regularly. There were monthly dances, a women's club (of which Baldwin was president), regular Monday night bridge games, visits from a public health nurse, and baby clinics. On Sundays there was an ecumenical Sunday School where Dawson Young served as superintendent for a few years. Young explained that schooling on the site was something of a problem. At first it was suggested that the children be sent to Loreburn, which was close to the site, but the school there could not accommodate them and they were bussed to Outlook instead. The buses where supplied and operated by PFRA and there were no tuition fees paid to the school, it being considered part of the larger school district.

As might be expected, the sudden influx of a substantial number of young men placed some strains on resources, particularly the local "watering hole." Conrad Romuld, in a report for the *Western Producer*, added flavour to his story by quoting snippets of conversation he overheard:

> At 8:30 on Thursday night the pub in Elbow had four customers, two farmers still summerfallow dusty and two men in oil company green.

However, by nine o'clock the room was full and an extra waiter had to come to help out.

The rush started with a noisy group of youths… . They were members of a construction camp ball team who had just lost their game. "What do you expect when you train on beer?"

There were eight at one table five at another each one shouting to make himself heard over the others.

The bartender, after questioning him about his age, refused to serve one discomfitted young man. "Hey, who'll lend George a birth certificate? You Dan? Not Dan he's only 19… Hey Dan Why is your face so red?"

New arrivals sat in, most of them construction workers. Most of them young. "I figured I was doin' 80, but the cops clocked me at 84. I didn't have no driver's licences either… Whose gonna pitch Sunday? … He was out with this girl and she was only 14 … at fifty she started to shimmy so I floorboarded her and the next thing I knew I was in the ditch."

A maintenance man on the project says that it's more dangerous to be on the access roads than it is on the job.[12]

However, while these shenanigans may seem a little robust, life as a whole was described as fairly civilized. J. Gordon Watson, chief engineer on the project at one time, said there were stringent rules written into the contracts governing the behaviour of the employees, as one young man found to his expense.

Dawson Young recounted the story of a young construction worker who was smitten by the young lady who lived next to Young in the PFRA headquarters compound. One night, in search of a glimpse of his true love, he drove by with his eyes rivetted on the young lady's residence instead of on where he was driving. Consequently, he plowed into the side of Young's car. In the ensuing investigation it was determined that the young driver did not have a driver's licence and was driving his brother's car, which was not properly licensed. The young man was fired on the spot. By the time he had paid for all the damage, he was left with $148 for a summer's work.

While the economic impact of the dam on the surrounding communities was considerable and quite expected, there was one particular economic boon that was quite unexpected: tourism. In the province as a whole and in regions beyond, the dam was a focus of great interest. One news report noted that the dam ranked third in tourist attractions during 1960, when officials recorded 82,550 visitors to the construction site. The following July, Harold Longman reported, 19,000 visitors registered at the PFRA pavilion during that single month.[13] This flood of visitors came from every province in Canada and every state in the United States, as well as the United Kingdom, Sweden, Denmark, Norway, Yugoslavia, Burma, China and Japan. However, the greatest number of visitors came from Saskatchewan, many returning regularly to check the progress of the work.[14]

A Rose by Any Other Name…

As the dams and creation of the reservoir neared completion, a new round of political in-fighting began, focussing on the naming of the dam and the lake.[15] At first glance, it is difficult to understand why the issue of the dam's name became so contentious. However, over the course of the decades preceding its construction, the dam became a focal point for Saskatchewan's ever-turbulent politics, and at one time or another, every major Saskatchewan political figure was involved.

At one point there was a suggestion to name the lake after Jimmy Gardiner's son, an RCAF pilot who had been killed over France. This idea was in keeping with the tradition of the provincial government to name certain geographical features after servicemen who had lost their lives in World War II. The Gardiner family, however, rejected the idea; they felt that if the deceased young airman was to have a lake named after him, it should be his alone, unsullied by the political squabbling that was going on.

Another early suggestion made by Alvin Hamilton (then leader of the Saskatchewan Conservatives and later Diefenbaker's minister of Agriculture) was J.R. MacNicol, Conservative member of

Parliament for Davenport, who had been vocal in his support of the project. Premier Douglas responded thus to Hamilton's request:

> Thank you for your letter of June 28 [1950], asking me to support your suggestion that if a dam is built on the South Saskatchewan it should be called the MacNicol Dam.
>
> It was my privilege to know Mr. MacNicol for some fifteen years and I have pleasant memories of his innumerable kindnesses to me when I was elected to the House of Commons as a new member in 1935. Mr. MacNicol took a great deal of interest in water conservation and was a constant champion of any project for conserving water one always counted upon to support irrigation projects on the prairies.
>
> Nevertheless, I doubt if it would be wise to associate his name with the Saskatchewan River Project. In the first place he was not intimately connected with the project and secondly, I don't think the name would mean much to Western Canadians, and particularly, the people of Saskatchewan.
>
> I know that what I am going to suggest will sound very strange, coming from me but I have had in the back of my mind for some time the idea that this dam, if it is proceeded with, ought to be called the Gardiner Dam. Mr. Gardiner has represented Saskatchewan in the Federal Cabinet continuously since 1935 and if the dam is completed, it will be in large part due to his efforts. I don't need to tell you that I have disagreed with Mr. Gardiner on almost every major item in domestic politics over the past 20 years. The fact remains, however, that by the time this dam is completed Mr. Gardiner will in all probability have retired from public life. It would be a fitting memorial to a man who has served the province both in provincial and federal affairs for more than a quarter of a century, to have his name associated with a project that is so essential to Saskatchewan Agriculture.[16]

Douglas's response is an indication that even some two decades before the completion of the project, the name Gardiner was an obvious choice to be considered when naming the dam. Yet the fact that the dam does bear his name probably has more to do with political timing than with the fact that the dam was completed, as Douglas said, "in large part due to his efforts." After all, the agreement to build the dam had been signed by John Diefenbaker and nearly the entire construction occurred during Diefenbaker's mandate. However, by the time the dam was nearing completion, the Liberals had been returned to power, federally under Lester Pearson *and* provincially under Ross Thatcher. Early in 1967, Pearson announced that the dam on the South Saskatchewan River would be known as the Gardiner Dam.[17]

While the dam had been named, this was not the end of the story. As Bill Barry notes in *People Places: Saskatchewan and Its Names*, "Diefenbaker complained — longly and loudly — about the iniquity of naming a dam for Jimmy Gardiner, and many people in Saskatchewan agreed with him."[18] His complaints did not go unheard. Ross Thatcher was something of a renegade, with little affinity for the federal branch of his party, and was primarily interested in improving his own chances of re-election. Hoping to win over Conservative supporters, Thatcher hit upon the idea of naming the lake behind the dam after John Diefenbaker.

Thatcher's involvement in the naming of the lake is revealed in two memos Diefenbaker wrote for his own records. The first, dated May 16, 1967, reads:

On Monday I talked with Premier Thatcher and told him I had in mind not to attend [the opening of the dam]. He seemed concerned over that because, as he told me on an earlier occasion, that he would not be able to go either unless I was present.

During the phone conversation he told me that a plan had been agreed to confidentially whereby the great lake created by the dam — the largest in Saskatchewan — would be named after me.[19]

The second memo was dated May 29, and continued in the same vein:

Today I talked with Premier Thatcher and advised him that I received his letter and that I would not be attending the Opening of the dam.

He said he was having difficulties with his colleagues and that they had decided in co-operation with Mr. Pearson that there should be a joint announcement.

The Prime Minister made the announcement regarding the naming the dam the Gardiner Dam and now is trying to find a way to show his broadmindedness.

He has nothing whatever to do with the naming of the Lake which falls entirely under jurisdiction of the Province.

He said it was still their intention to name it Diefenbaker Lake.

I said that would not alter my stand one bit.

I said I would make it known in advance that I would not be there under the circumstances.

I said if he made the announcement I

Scenes from the official opening of the completed project on July 21, 1967:

Facing page: leaders and former leaders — the political backbiting and infighting forgotten for the moment — are all smiles as the historical plaque at the site is unveiled. From left to right, former Saskatchewan premier, T.C. Douglas; then Saskatchewan premier, Ross Thatcher; former prime minister, John Diefenbaker, then prime minister, Lester Pearson.
Photo courtesy SAB — R-B4478(2).

Above: the commemorative plaque unveiled at the site recognizes the key persons and agencies whose work — whether political, administrative, or scientific — resulted in the completion of the South Saskatchewan River Project.
Photo courtesy SAB — R-A28195.

Left: Thousands attend the official opening, an occasion made all the more festive because it took place in the nation's centennial year.
Photo courtesy SAB — R-A28196.

would have immediately stated that he had nothing to with the naming of the dam, that that was the action of the Prime Minister.[20]

On the eve of the opening of the dam and the lake, Thatcher unilaterally announced that the lake would indeed bear Diefenbaker's name, since he had been prime minister when the agreement for construction of the Gardiner Dam was signed.[21]

Despite his protestations to the contrary less than two months earlier, Diefenbaker had a sudden change of heart and appeared at the opening in fine fettle. In his typical, high-flown rhetoric, "The Chief" announced that the "completion of the dam was a triumph over people of faint heart who had ridiculed and condemned the idea."[22]

It was also reported that Diefenbaker managed to get in ten minutes of fishing. Dr. Lewis Brand, a Saskatoon member of Parliament, was given the dubious honour of carrying Diefenbaker's rod and reel. As soon as the fishing gear was handed to him, Diefenbaker got into action, and almost immediately hauled from his namesake lake a fine, fat Northern Pike. Though there was no visible evidence of a fence or fish pen, the speed with which he landed the fish raised eyebrows. Had something been rigged to assure Diefenbaker's success? The author, who accompanied Brand, always felt there was something "fishy" about the whole incident.

The following ten pages provide a brief pictorial account of the changing face of the dam site as construction proceeded on the South Saskatchewan River Project from 1958 to 1967.

Left and below: Winter and summer drilling by PFRA on the South Saskatchewan River.
Photo left courtesy SAB — R-A27026(1).
Photo below courtesy SAB — R-A27027(2).

Photo left courtesy SAB — R-B5547-14.

Photo right courtesy SAB — R-B13126.

Left: Aerial views of the dam and town site (1959).
Photo courtesy SAB — R-B8562-2.

Below: Aerial view as construction proceeds.
Photo courtesy SAB — R-B13129.

Above: Closing the South Saskatchewan River dam, February 1964.
Photo courtesy SAB — R-A16437(7)

Right: Dr. George Spence, first director of PFRA, at the closing of the South Saskatchewan River dam, February 1964.
Photo courtesy SAB — R-A16435(1).

Low-level and high-level intake structures were constructed between 1964 and 1966.

Facing Page: Left: Photo courtesy SAB — R-B12780(4).
Right, top: Photo courtesy SAB — R-B12055(2).
Right, bottom: Photo courtesy SAB — R-A16436(4).

Right: low-level intake structures.
Photo courtesy SAB — R-A16436(1).

Below: A dragline at work near the intake structures.
Photo courtesy SAB — R-A16436 (3).

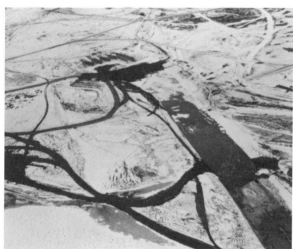

Aerial photos of the dam:
Above: Tunnel outlets and spillway, February 1964.
Photo courtesy SAB — R-A16439(2).

Above: Aerial view of the dam site showing spillway, control shafts, high level intakes, 1966.
Photo courtesy SAB — R-B4318(4).

Right: Aerial view of the low-level and high-level intake structures, February 1964.
Photo courtesy SAB – - R-A16436(2).

SOUTH SASKATCHEWAN
RIVER DAMSITE

*The South Saskatchewan
River from the air "Before"
and "After" the project.*

*Left: The South
Saskatchewan River as it
looked in 1958. The arrows
show the site of the dam.
Photo courtesy SAB —
R-B4318(1).*

Right: the completed dam. White lettering shows construction headquarters, tunnel control shafts, tunnel outlet and powerhouse, spillway and east side pumping plant.
Photo courtesy SAB — R-A28202.

A model of the dam site with significant components labelled:

1. PFRA Headquarters
2. Contractor's Camp
3. Observation Point
4. Stage I Embankment
5. Construction Bridge
6. River Closure Section
7. Stage II Embankment
8. Upstream Waste Berm
9. Tunnel Inlets
10. High Level Intakes
11. Control Shafts
12. Tunnel Outlets
13. Spillway Approach Channel
14. Spillway Excavation
15. Stage III Embankment
16. Concrete Aggregate Stockpiles
17. Ring Beam Stockpiles
18. Tunnel Liner Storage

Photo courtesy SAB — R-B12056.

84

— SEVEN —

Bringing in the Sheaves

A new wave of pioneers were lined up and ready to begin an exciting new adventure even before the dam was officially opened. Five farmers had each levelled 34 acres by the fall of 1966: J.P. and Art Hauberg, Elmer Niska, and Edgar and Arnold Carlson. The Carlsons were imbued with the same pioneering spirit, although on a much grander scale, that their father, Anton, had brought with him from Sweden. In the application for title to his homestead in 1906, his assets were meager: two oxen, a sod stable valued at $40, a 10x12 house valued at $80. Of the 17 acres he had broken, he cropped 12. In contrast to these scant holdings, the two brothers had amassed several hundred acres.

The first demonstration of irrigation took place on Arnold Carlson's 34 acres and attracted about 100 spectators; by the following year he had 300 acres under irrigation. From this humble beginning, which was seen by many as risky, irrigation would flourish, and by the end of 1997, 435 farmers would be using this method to get water onto over 100,000 acres of land.

Praise for Project

Both of the Carlson brothers praised the project, stating that they had favoured irrigation right from the start. Both grew up in the 1930s, and were thus ingrained with a special appreciation of water. Some three decades later, they had no regrets.

Arnold Carlson told the author, in the summer of 1994, that from the very beginning he had encountered no problems with irrigation: "It worked like a charm. Today I would never go farming without water, NEVER!" Brother Edgar echoed this sentiment, proclaiming that irrigation was "the best thing that ever happened to my family."

Both men also praised the Liberal government of then-premier Ross Thatcher, which had been particularly helpful in tiding them over during the difficult transition period. About two years after start-up, the five farmers involved in the initial irrigation systems were having a bit of difficulty balancing income from the crops with the costs of capital investment and the intricacies of moving from dryland to irrigation farming. They decided they should take their plight to the top and arranged an interview with Thatcher. They were modest in their requests and suggested that something in the nature of $10 per acre might see them through. Thatcher acted quickly, and within a few weeks they had their money, thus averting what Arnold Carlson thought was a potentially disastrous situation.

Missteps

The course of progress did not, however, always flow smoothly. As Edgar Carlson noted, mistakes were sometimes made. In the first place, he initially miscalculated the use of water, feeling that if one gallon was good then two gallons would surely be better. Unfortunately, things did not work out quite that way. If the water table is raised too much, it brings salt up with it and salinity becomes a problem.

Some years later, Edgar Carlson moved to a farm north of Broderick. There he made another miscalculation. He paid $89,000 for a quarter section of land with flood irrigation already in place.

However, he felt that "I'd have been better off if it hadn't been in. I had to take it out." One of his sons started to experiment with some grass mixes on the unproductive land and within a year or two it started to recover and by the summer of 1994 it was again producing well.

Two other enterprises cost Carlson "a lot of bucks." One was an alfalfa cubing venture, another was a potato operation in a co-operative involving about twenty farmers. These failed because, he said bluntly, "We didn't know what the hell we were doing." The potato venture was slow in getting established because the quality of the potatoes was poor, and the costs of planting, harvesting, storage and rent on the land they were leasing from the government were greater than profits. The alfalfa project encountered similar problems in the beginning, and for a time it appeared that the venture would never be a success. Experience, however, proved to be a good teacher in both cases, and by the end of 1997, after going through three owners, the cubing plant was thriving and the potato industry was booming.

Hamilton's Progress

Another adventurer was the late Tommy Hamilton, who was the first to install a centre-pivot irrigation system in the region. He said during an interview in 1992 that word reached him that some of his neighbours thought he was crazy, as they stood on a hill overlooking his installation. He added dryly that "Before I had it up and running, at times I thought they just might be right."

While setting up his own pumps and drawing water from the lake for his new method of water distribution may have looked foolhardy to some, Hamilton felt that he was being cautious. The total cost was approximately $25,000, which he considered manageable. The system covered 140 acres which he seeded to alfalfa to provide forage for his 900 head of cattle. Hamilton refused to act precipitately, stating that "I let one pivot pay for the next." By 1992 he had ten pivots covering 1,400 acres and proudly proclaimed: "I've never had a crop failure on irrigated land." He was quick to acknowledge his indebtedness to the SSRP, stating that he owed most of his success to the water supply drawn from Lake Diefenbaker.

Hamilton's foresight was proven over the course of time, and the system he pioneered in the 1960s came to be widely adopted. By 1992, of 320,000 acres under irrigation in Saskatchewan, 109,000 employed pivot systems.

Unfortunately, not all farmers were as successful as Hamilton and the Carlsons. Ken Hall, who started farming at the age of 18, told the author that "By the time I decided to throw in the towel, I had five quarters, with 400 acres under irrigation. I had been growing wheat, hard spring red both on dryland and on irrigated land. I also grew canary seed, rye, durum and oats." In essence he said the problem that he faced was that the costs of farming exceeded income. His land was at a higher elevation and costs of irrigation were thus more than expected.

Faced with mounting debts, Hall was forced to dispose of his farm, eventually relocating to Castlegar, where he opened a pawn shop. Nevertheless, while glad that he gave up farming, Hall still believes the creation of Lake Diefenbaker "balances out as a good thing." He noted, in particular, the great advances made in potato operations in the Lucky Lake area, the fish farm in the same region, and the successful piggeries which have been established.

Hall was not alone in being unable to successfully adapt to irrigation farming. According to data collected by Paul Brassard of the Rural Life Ministry, near 30 percent of the farmers in the area had financial problems so acute that they were obliged to turn to one or the other of two agencies — the federally sponsored Farm Debt Review Board, and the provincially administered Farm Act Security Board — set up to help farmers.

In the federal case, part of legislation specified that there must be a 120-day notice served on farmers before land was seized for debt. This period allowed time for further negotiation and an opportunity for farmers to liquidate a portion of their assets to pay off some of the debt. On the provincial front, provisions were made for negotiation and, until 1992, the lender was required to offer a lease-back of land either given up voluntarily or seized to cover debts. Besides this, the Farm Act

Security Board offered advice, short of legal counsel, to farmers working their way through problems of land-debt load. Two brothers, Robert and Merle Larson, are a case in point. They farm 2,000 acres of their own land plus another 1,000 acres under lease. They started irrigating in 1972, after "giving it a real hard look."

In their opinion, it was the early compulsive nature of implementing irrigation which led to problems in later years. In the course of their experience, dating from 1946, they had grown alfalfa, potatoes (on contract), canary seed (which they abandoned after one year when yields were poor), pinto beans, faba beans, lentils, and canola. During this time, they ran into some financial problems and went to the Farm Debt Revue Board. Both felt the experience was "great." They voluntarily relinquished a portion of their land to cover their indebtedness. The bank then leased it back to them until they could get their financial affairs in order. They were then allowed to buy the land back at what they described as "a very fair price." By 1993 they had it all paid off.

Dan Patterson, Manager of the Farm Act Security Board, says that most such claims were handled in a similar manner, noting that in the province as a whole, lenders were in possession of one million acres of farm land in November 1997, down from three million a few years earlier.

An Oasis for a Desert

Mint

The advent of irrigation allowed area farmers to experiment with a variety of new crops which hitherto could not be grown. One of these was mint.

Plains Investments (PI) of Saskatoon, a trading company dealing in lentils and canola, had a British partner which had purchased a perfume company and was searching for a source of natural oils (oils which are used for their flavours and fragrances). Plains Investments was asked to help in the search, and eventually decided to experiment with mint.

In 1989, PI conducted a market study which indicated there were possibilities in this niche market. PI then took the process a step further by examining samples in the laboratory and then in a greenhouse. Finally, PI contacted the Saskatchewan Irrigation Development Centre and seeded a half-acre test plot, with promising results; the next year 25 acres were seeded. By 1994, PI was satisfied that mint was a marketable commodity, and made arrangements with ten farmers to seed 1,070 acres. Simultaneously, a processing plant was built in Elbow, which at peak season employs about 20 persons. The output of this plant is exported to the United States, the United Kingdom, Western Europe, and Japan, where it is used for air fresheners, toothpaste, mouthwash and chewing gum.

Glen Gordon, one of the principals in the company, noted that diversification had long been advocated by community leaders, but that little progress had yet been made. The mint operation, however, was a bold first step in this direction, and Gordon was confident that its success would encourage other entrepreneurs to experiment with new products.

Potatoes

One of the more exciting of irrigation-related enterprises was the rapid expansion of the potato industry in the Lucky Lake

A field of potatoes under irrigation due to the South Saskatchewan River Project. Photo courtesy SaskWater.

area. Early in the development stages of Lake Diefenbaker a Manitoba company moved into the region and established a potato operation. Within a couple of years, they gave it up as unprofitable. The operation was taken over by Barrich Farms, and this time it proved successful.

Bill Childerhose, one-time mayor of Outlook, had abandoned a banking career to help form Barrich Farms. He believed that the decision to lease land, rather than face the large capital investment of purchasing it, was one of the keys to the success of the operation. By the early 1990s Barrich Farms was producing some 8,000 tons of potatoes annually.

The company subsequently formed a marketing division, which dealt primarily with retail stores and some wholesale houses. A drying facility, capable of turning culls into starch which can be used in the potash industry (and which can also dry alfalfa for cubing), was established late in the 1990s. However, Harry Meyers, the third partner in the group, said that this component was being reconsidered because its small scale made commercial viability problematic.

Also in the early 1990s two Idaho potato farmers arrived in Lucky Lake. They were drawn to Saskatchewan by reports of a phenomenon known as "northern vigour." Basically, this meant that potatoes planted in the disease-free lands of more northerly climates had better yields. The two entrepreneurs planted some seed potatoes in a small plot, and took the new potatoes back to Idaho that fall. These were then seeded in Idaho the following spring, and it was found that, indeed, yields increased by 20 percent. Based on this surprising finding, the two men helped establish a company under the name of SaskIda.

According to Doug Barker, who at the time was manager of the Coteau Hills Rural Development Corporation, twenty-five local irrigation farmers put up $200,000, another $200,000 came through a grant from Saskatchewan Irrigation Based Economic Development (funded jointly by the Saskatchewan and federal governments) and another $400,000 was raised through bank loans. This $800,000 provided the capital for the establishment of the Coteau Potato Corporation. This corporation provided storage facilities, seeding and harvesting equipment. SaskIda's role was the provision of expertise, the seeding and harvesting, and marketing. In 1994, 640 acres of potatoes were seeded, on farm land leased from farmers (many of whom were shareholders in the potato corporation). When harvest came, the producers encountered an unanticipated — but pleasant — problem. Yields were far higher than expected, and there was a scramble for storage space. It was necessary to rent the curling rink in Riverhurst, which was quickly filled with potatoes. The product was then trucked into Washington, Oregon, Idaho, and Mexico. Business was brisk. The following year only 540 acres were seeded in order to meet the capacity of the storage facilities.

As time went on, the two founders of this development ran into financial problems back in Idaho and SaskIda closed. The people involved in Canada quickly set about a salvage mission and formed the Lake Diefenbaker Potato Corporation. The new structure now includes a partnership with Judith River Farms in Alberta and has close ties with the Coteau Hills Potato Corporation (Coteau rolled its assets into Lake Diefenbaker in return for shares in that entity). By 1997 the corporation had acquired new storage facilities and 2,500 acres were seeded. Barker, now marketing manager for the new corporation, predicted they would seed 5,700 acres in 1998, involving 25 farmers.

Meanwhile, the Lake Diefenbaker corporation shifted some of its focus from seed potatoes to the table potato market. In 1997, 600 tons of table potatoes were boxed, bagged and distributed through a broker to outlets such as Extra Foods, Superstore and Co-Op.

The new storage facilities were built courtesy of Spudco, a division of SaskWater, in the summer of 1997. The Lake Diefenbaker Potato Corporation leased the three new buildings from Spudco with an option to buy.

Harvey Fjeld, vice-president of Irrigation and Agriculture Products with SaskWater, explained that Spudco was formed to make better use of irrigation services by encouraging expansion in the potato industry to a point that there would be sufficient production to attract a french fry plant to the area.

This, he said, "could happen, if all goes well, by 2000 to 2002." In essence this goal would be achieved by Spudco partnering with potato growers as was done in the Lucky Lake area. Fjeld predicts that by the years 2000-2002, some 20,000 acres could be seeded.

At the same time, special attention was being paid to the potato industry by an agency which had an unusual history, in the sense it was established about ten years in advance of any concrete steps being taken toward the building of the dam.

In 1949 the Prairie Farm Rehabilitation Administration purchased 200 acres of land from the town of Outlook for $5. PFRA then proceeded to establish a pre-development farm on the property in order to introduce farmers to the intricacies of irrigation farming. Today it is jointly funded by SaskWater and PFRA. The name has been changed to the Saskatchewan Irrigation Development Centre and concentrates on the testing of new crops through a process which includes experimenting with crops on small plots on the property and then moving to plots of 8-10 acres on farms.

Laurie Tollefson, manager of the operation, explains that the direction of the agency has shifted into the realm of research and development. Tollefson reported early in 1998 that his researchers were spending a great deal of time working on variations in the potato industry with studies on the use of watering practices, the application of herbicides, pesticides and fertilizers on the sugar content, size, and texture of potato crops.[1]

Hogs

Another enterprise with an unusual history is a hog operation headed by Wayne Vermette. Vermette originally farmed in the Kyle area with his father, a long-time registered seed grower, but decided to get into livestock and particularly hogs.

Vermette explained that a 600-sow operation required some 15,000 gallons of water a day. However, the severe drought in the late 1980s made this impossible:

I thought I could collect that kind of volume through a series of dams and dugouts. But in 1988 there wasn't any moisture to collect and we wound up hauling water at the rate of 2,000 gallons a day. That opened my eyes to the fact that I could not expand in that [Kyle] area because I could not depend on these dams and dugouts to store the volume of water I needed.

Vermette and his three partners looked for a suitable location to relocate their operation, and eventually picked a site northeast of Outlook. They bought a half section of land and carried out soil and engineering studies. The whole process was then reviewed by five different branches of government: environment, water, health, the local rural municipality, and the Department of Agriculture and Food. The report came back "squeaky clean" and Agriculture and Food issued a permit to proceed.

Vermette continued:

Now we had bought the land, all studies were complete and we were within a week of starting construction when the permit was pulled. This came about through the vociferous lobbying on the part of a few farmers who lived nearby. We had a substantial investment in the project by this time and when the permit was pulled the investment vanished.

I got the impression that there was a lot of politics involved. I also heard that some bureaucrat in Regina had fumbled the ball by pulling the permit. I am not sure if that is true. Then I got a call from down south of Outlook from guys trying to help us out. There were 3,000 acres of pasture land down there owned by the Province and leased to a group of farmers who formed the Macrorie Grazing Co-op.

Under the terms of the lease, the Macrorie Grazing Co-op had to relinquish its interests before anything further could be done with the land.

A meeting was called with the stakeholders and before the afternoon was over, Vermette's Elite Stock Farm had a deal for a new parcel of land of about 190 acres. "Things moved quickly after that," Vermette said, though there was still an environmental review to go through before final approval would come. A report submitted by the PFRA's Environmental Studies Division in March 1990 stated that of 287 written comments on the proposals, 86 percent supported the project, 11 percent were opposed and 3 percent were undecided. The report also noted that "the socio-economic assessment concludes that the construction of Elite Stock Farm would create 44 person years of employment and generate $2.9 million of value added economic activity annually." It concluded that the Elite proposal would be acceptable from a federal environmental point of view.

Vermette explained that he was buying grain directly from the producer and Arnold Carlson, a nearby farmer, who sold to him said the price was a few cents a bushel higher than they got at the elevator. This proved to be an unexpected boon, for it qualified Vermette for a grant through Saskatchewan Irrigation Based Economic Development (SIBED), a federal-provincial agreement aimed at encouraging the expansion of irrigation. This agency provided 25 percent of the capital cost.

Ultimately, Vermette and his partners, Garth Larson and Richard Wright, started a company called Quadra, which provided consultative services to farmers wanting to get into the hog business. By early 1998, Quadra was firmly established as a management company and had ten plants in various parts of Saskatchewan and one in Manitoba; collectively, these plants house 8,400 sows.

Fish

The creation of Diefenbaker Lake led to the development of an unlikely industry in the middle of the prairies — fishing.

The Arctic Fish Company was started in Waldheim by John Beilka, and was purchased by AgPro, a division of the Saskatchewan Wheat Pool. It was decided to locate the company at Lake Diefenbaker, but several years of negotiations were involved — with the provincial departments of Health and Environment, and the federal departments of Fisheries and Oceans, and Canada Transport, which was responsible for enforcing regulations of the navigable *Waters Protection Act*. There were some strict guidelines imposed on the operation including regular water-quality tests, sediment sampling and chemical analysis. The Department of Environment and Public Safety appeared to be satisfied that that all necessary precautions were being taken, and the project was approved on May 7, 1992.

The results have been gratifying. Twice a week, on chilly winter mornings, refrigerated trucks load up at the site just east of Lucky Lake and head to Vancouver, Seattle or New York. Early in 1998, the company was shipping about 200,000 pounds per year of Rainbow Trout fillets, and employed some sixty workers. Other fish species have been introduced, including Atlantic Salmon and Arctic Char, but Lake Diefenbaker is too warm in summer for these species to develop properly.

There has been one unanticipated problem in the development of this industry. Garnet Wendell, assistant operations manager, explained that irresponsible sport fishermen have had a detrimental impact on the operation. Many so-called sport fishermen would pull up to one of the thirty pens in which the fish were held and cast into them. They also trolled around the pens and hurled insults at the workers as they were passing by to feed the fish or repair the nets. Eventually a law was passed specifying the distance the fishermen must keep back from the pens, but infractions still occur.

Alfalfa Cubing

The alfalfa cubing plant just north of Broderick had a troubled history, going through three sets of owners before being purchased by Hartley and Greg Sommerfeld and Ron Butterly. The company, know as Elcan Forage, buys raw stock from about 800 farmers on a daily quoted price. The business has grown steadily, and in 1998 it was exporting approximately 30,000 tonnes per year, mainly to Pacific Rim countries.

Greg Sommerfeld noted that the company was actively endeavouring to expand its market base into the United States. It is currently installing equipment to produce mixed feeds rather than straight alfalfa forage, which Sommerfeld says is aimed at broadening the market base.

Epilogue

Was it all worthwhile? Were the decades of political negotiation and infighting involved in the South Saskatchewan River Project worth a dam(n)? In retrospect, some thirty years after the dam's completion, a review of its impact — both geographical and economical — is in order.

Of the impact of the SSRP on the environment, there is no doubt. While construction was underway, the site housed the largest implement workshop in Canada (measuring 180 feet by 130 feet). Under the auspices of McNamara Construction, there were 49 earth buggies (each capable of moving up to 27 cubic feet of earth) and 25 caterpillar tractors involved, all of them serviced on site.[1] The end result was

> the construction of a dam impound[ing] 8,000,000 acre feet of water, or enough to cover 8,000,000 acres to a depth of one foot. ... 140 miles long, 180 feet deep at the dam and [with a] shore line of 475 miles. The flooded area at full supply level [would] be approximately 109,600 acres, 5.2% of which [was then] under cultivation. The remaining land immediately

adjacent to the river ha[d] little agricultural value.

The South Saskatchewan River Dam [would] be the largest rolled-earth dam ever built in Canada and one of the larger dams of its kind in the world.

The amount of excavation required to build the dam would make a hole in the ground a city block square 1½ miles deep. Enough steel [would] be used in the dam to make a 3/8" steel rod long enough to stretch around the earth.

The cement needed would fill to capacity 3,000 freight cars.

The concrete used would build a two-lane super highway from Regina to Prince Albert in Saskatchewan, a distance of approximately 225 miles.

The diversion tunnels [would] be large enough for a train to pass through.

The irrigable area was estimated at 500,000 acres.[2]

The economic impact of the dam on Saskatchewan was equally staggering. For example, the construction costs of the South Saskatchewan River Project amounted to $120 million[3] (in 1999 figures, this would be close to $1 billion). Most of this money was spent in the province and provided a tremendous boost to the provincial economy.

Nor did the economic benefits end when the construction crews left. As was noted in Chapter 7, the appearance of Gardiner Dam and Diefenbaker Lake led to many new or expanded agricultural endeavours in the area based on irrigation. Furthermore, tourism boomed. And, last but by no means least, over 50% of the provincial population was guaranteed a reliable supply of clean water, for both domestic and industrial use.

Brad Fairley, who headed a 1990 federal government review of the SSRP, was unequivocal in his praise: "There have been some very bad dams built [but] construction of the Gardiner dam was one of the smartest things the province ever did."[4]

The benefits of the dam, as is evident in another study commissioned by the Canadian government and published in 1988, were both economic and environmental:

> [It had] a total value of direct benefits of $2,038 million in 1986 dollars. The present value of direct costs is estimated at $1,909 million. The net direct benefit to society is thus $129 million.
>
> …
>
> The project has brought land, water and human resources together to provide a productive and aesthetically pleasing environment that would otherwise not exist. This enhances and increases conservation projects of plants, wildlife, waterfowl and fish habitat.[5]

To put a slightly more human face on a project which sometimes, by its sheer size, has dwarfed human concerns, let us close with an observation made by a young woman some time before construction of the dam started. Living in a community which hitherto lacked the benefits of indoor plumbing, she noted pithily: "Any project that keeps my tender bottom off the seat of an outdoor privy at forty below is worth every cent no matter what the cost."

Notes

Chapter One

1. John Palliser, *Papers Relative to the Exploration by Captain John Palliser* (London: Queen's Printers, 1859), 74.

2. Ibid.

3. John Macoun, *Autobiography* (Ottawa: The Ottawa Field Naturalists Club, 1922), 204.

4. Saskatchewan Archives Board (SAB), James G. Gardiner Papers, R1022 VI -2.

5. Ibid.

6. Edgar Carlson, interview with the author, 1995.

7. Roslyn A. Case and Glen M. MacDonald, "A Dendroclimatic Reconstruction of Annual Precipitation on the Western Canadian Prairies Since A.D. 1505 from *Pinus flexilis* James" *Quartenary Research* 44:2 (September 1995): 267-275.

8. John H. Archer, *Saskatchewan: A History* (Saskatoon: Western Producer Prairie Books, 1963), 56.

9. Chester Martin, *"Dominion Lands" Policy* (1938; Toronto: Macmillan, 1973), 148.

10. T.H. Hogg et al., *Report of the Royal Commission on the South Saskatchewan River Project* (Ottawa: Queen's Printer, 1952), 106-07.

11. Archer, *Saskatchewan*, 392.

12. Quoted in Martin, *"Dominion Lands" Policy*, 420.

13. Arthur S. Morton, *History of Prairie Settlement* (Toronto: Macmillan, 1938), 144.

14. Regina *Leader-Post*, November 25, 1995.

15. Henry Youle Hind, *Canadian Red River and Assiniboine and Saskatchewan Expeditions*, vol. 1 (London: Longman, Green, Longman and Roberts, 1860), 428.

16. Ibid., 429.

17. George Spence, *Survival of a Vision* (Ottawa: Queen's Printer, 1967), 17-18.

18. Ibid., 18.

19. Ibid., 18-19.

20. Ibid., 37.

21. Ibid., 32.

22. Ibid., 44.

Chapter Two

1. The spelling and punctuation are those of the writer.

2. Michael Horn (ed.), *The Dirty Thirties* (Toronto: Copp Clark, 1972), 232-33.

3. T.H. Hogg et al., *Report of the Royal Commission on the South Saskatchewan River Project* (Ottawa: Queen's Printer, 1952), 298.

4. A.S. Morton, *History of Prairie Settlement* (Toronto: Macmillan, 1938), xvi.

5. R.B. Godwin, "Twenty droughts in the Canadian Prairies in the Nineteenth Century " in D.J. Bauer (ed.), *Proceedings of the Prairie Drought Workshop*, Saskatoon, Saskatchewan, October 11-13, 1988 (Ottawa: Environment Canada, 1989), 11.

6. James H. Gray, *The Winter Years* (Toronto: Macmillan, 1966), 166.

7. Saskatchewan Archives Board (SAB), James G. Gardiner Papers, 27089.

8. SAB, James G. Gardiner Papers, 1022 VII 2a. 2604-39.

9. James H. Gray, *Men Against the Desert* (Saskatoon: Western Producer Prairie Books, 1967), 225.

10. George Spence, *Survival of a Vision* (Ottawa: Queen's Printer, 1967), 91-92.

11. Ibid., 97.

12. Ibid., 101.

13. Ibid., 124-25.

14. Ibid., 125-26.

15. Ibid., 130.

Chapter Three

1. Saskatchewan Archives Board (SAB), SSRDA papers, R160 III-1.

2. Ibid.

3. Ibid.

4. L.B. Thomson was instilled with a sense of mission about the South Saskatchewan River Project which at least equalled that of Spence. A former New Zealander, he had arrived in Canada in 1920 and landed a job as sheep shearer. He later entered Olds Agricultural College, which he followed with a degree in agriculture from the University of Alberta. By 1935 he was head of the Dominion Experimental Station in Swift Current and closely linked to PFRA's rehabilitation efforts.

5. SAB, T.C. Douglas papers, R33.1 I, James G. Gardiner papers, R1022 VII 2a.

6. T.H. Hogg et al., *Report of the Royal Commission on the South Saskatchewan River Project* (Ottawa: Queen's Printer, 1952), 1.

7. Regina *Leader-Post*, September 9, 1952.

8. Hogg, *Report of the Royal Commission,* 298.

9. Ibid., 300-1.

10. Ibid., 6-7.

11. "Saskatchewan Replies to the Royal Commission on the SSRP," Queen's Printer, Regina, 1953.

12. Ibid.

13. Ibid.

14. Ibid.

15. Ibid.

16. SAB, James G. Gardiner papers, R1022 VII 2a. 26504-39

17. Ibid.

18. Ibid.

19. Ibid.

20. Dale C. Thompson, *Louis St. Laurent: Canadian* (Toronto, MacMillan, 1967), 507.

21. SAB, T.C. Douglas Papers, GR 90-1 R33-18.

Chapter Four

1. Diefenbaker Centre Archives, John G. Diefenbaker Fonds, MG 01/XI/C/405, Vol. 76.

2. Ibid., VI/1048, Vol. 84.

3. In a Hansard entry for March 29, 1949, he listed all the benefits of the project and closed with this observation: "What the prairie provinces demand is not the doing of this work which indicates that it is a lifelong project, but that it be proceeded with immediately and completed in accordance with the best energy that the engineers may devote to its completion."

4. Diefenbaker Centre Archives, John G. Diefenbaker Fonds, 752.641, Vol. 526, file 8288.1, 401209.

5. Ibid., 8882.2 401599

6. Ibid.

7. Ibid. 401567.

8. Regina *Leader-Post*, July 2, 1958.

9. Diefenbaker Centre Archives, John G. Diefenbaker Fonds, 752.641, Vol. 526, file 8882.2, 401541.

10. Saskatchewan Archives Board (SAB), T.C. Douglas papers, R33-1-I-19-1

11. *Financial Post*, June 6, 1959.

Chapter Five

1. Interview with Mr. and Mrs. Arlo Larson and minutes of meeting in their possession.
2. Saskatoon *Star-Phoenix*, October 22, 1965.
3. Reported in the *Western Producer*, March 25,1965.
4. Interview with Mr. and Mrs. Arlo Larson and minutes of meeting in their possession.
5. Saskatoon *Star-Phoenix*, October 25, 1965.
6. PFRA Library, HD 1696 S3 15, Barcode 15521.
7. Ibid.
8. Ibid.
9. Ibid.
10. Ibid.
11. Ibid.
12. PFRA correspondence files.

Chapter Six

1. Regina *Leader-Post*, October 2, 1958.
2. Ibid.
3. Conrad Romuld, *Western Producer*, May 14, 1964.
4. Longman, Regina *Leader-Post*, October 2, 1958.
5. Ibid.
6. Ibid., October 2, 1961.
7. Copy of report in the possession of J. Gordon Watson, former director of PFRA, Regina.
8. Romuld, *Western Producer*, April 30, 1964.

9. Ibid., May 7, 1964.

10. Ibid., April 30, 1964.

11. *Design and Construction of Gardiner Dam and Associated Works* (Canada: Prairie Farm Rehabilitation Administration, 1980), 213.

12. Romuld, *Western Producer*, May 7, 1964.

13. Longman, *Leader-Post*.

14. *The Financial Post*, October 21, 1961.

15. Davey Steuart was a long-time member of Ross Thatcher's Liberal government, which was in power at the time of the dam's completion. When asked about the toughest part of the project, Steuart's response was: "We had a hell of a fight over naming the thing."

16. SAB, T.C. Douglas Papers, R33.1 I-19.

17. Sadly, Jimmy Gardiner had died in 1962, four years before the announcement that the dam would bear his name. Prime Minister Pearson saw the naming of the dam "as fitting recognition to a man who played a leading role in the development of Saskatchewan, and whose foresight and faith in his province contributed immeasurably to the harnessing of the South Saskatchewan."

18. Bill Barry, *People Places: Saskatchewan and Its Names* (Regina: Canadian Plains Research Center, 1997), 99.

19. DCA, John Diefenbaker fonds, MG 01/XII/F/440/ vol. 123.

20. Ibid., XIV/E/232.

21. In an apparent effort to appease voters of every political persuasion, Thatcher also announced that a large park bordering the lake would be named after T.C. Douglas, who had, of course, been premier when the agreement was signed between the two governments and who had been a constant supporter of the project.

22. Saskatoon *Star-Phoenix*, July 22, 1967.

Chapter Seven

1. The story of commercial market gardening of potatoes in the area continues to unfold. In 1999, the latest in the series of potatoe ventures, which had been heavily subsidized by the government of Saskatchewan, had declared bankruptcy. At the time of publication, the case was before the bankruptcy courts.

Epilogue

1. Regina *Leader-Post*, November 7, 1964.

2. DCA, John Diefenbaker Fonds, MG01/viiE/125pp 18177-18181.

3. *Design and Construction of Gardiner Dam and Associated Works* (Canada: Prairie Farm Rehabilitation Administration, 1980), iii.

4. Brad Fairley, *Ground Water and the South Saskatchewan River Basin Study: Recommendations to the Study Board* (Canada-Saskatchewan: South Saskatchewan River Basin Study Office, 1988).

5. Suren Kulshreshtha, K. Dale Russell and Kurt K. Klein, *Social Evaluation of the South Saskatchewan River Project* (Ottawa: Queen's Printer, 1988).